JAILED BY BLOOD: INMATE 798175

By
Quiet Storm

Esquire Publications
P. O. Box 61904
Harrisburg, PA 17106
www.esquirepublications.com
Tel: (800) 501-7640

"Jailed By Blood: Inmate 798175"

Copyright © 2010 by Quiet Storm

Edited By: Georgia Editing Service, LLC –
www.georgiaeditingservicellc.com

Design By: Designs Unparallel, LLC – www.designsunparallel.net

This book is a work of nonfiction. All rights reserved. No part of this book may be reproduced or transmitted in any form or by any means, electronic or mechanical, including photocopying and recording, or by any information storage and retrieval system, without permission in writing from the publisher.

First Edition February 2009
Second Edition April 2010
Third Edition February 2011

Library of Congress Cataloging-in-Publication Data

Library of Congress Control Number: 2010923297

ISBN: 9780982669020

Printed in the United States of America

PREFACE

But [when these men set a trap for others] they are lying in wait for their own blood; they set an ambush for their own lives.

Proverbs 1:18

Quiet Storm: May 2007

A Special Dedication To:

"Feisty Midget"

"Sleeping Beauty"

"Goldie"

JAILED BY BLOOD: INMATE 79817

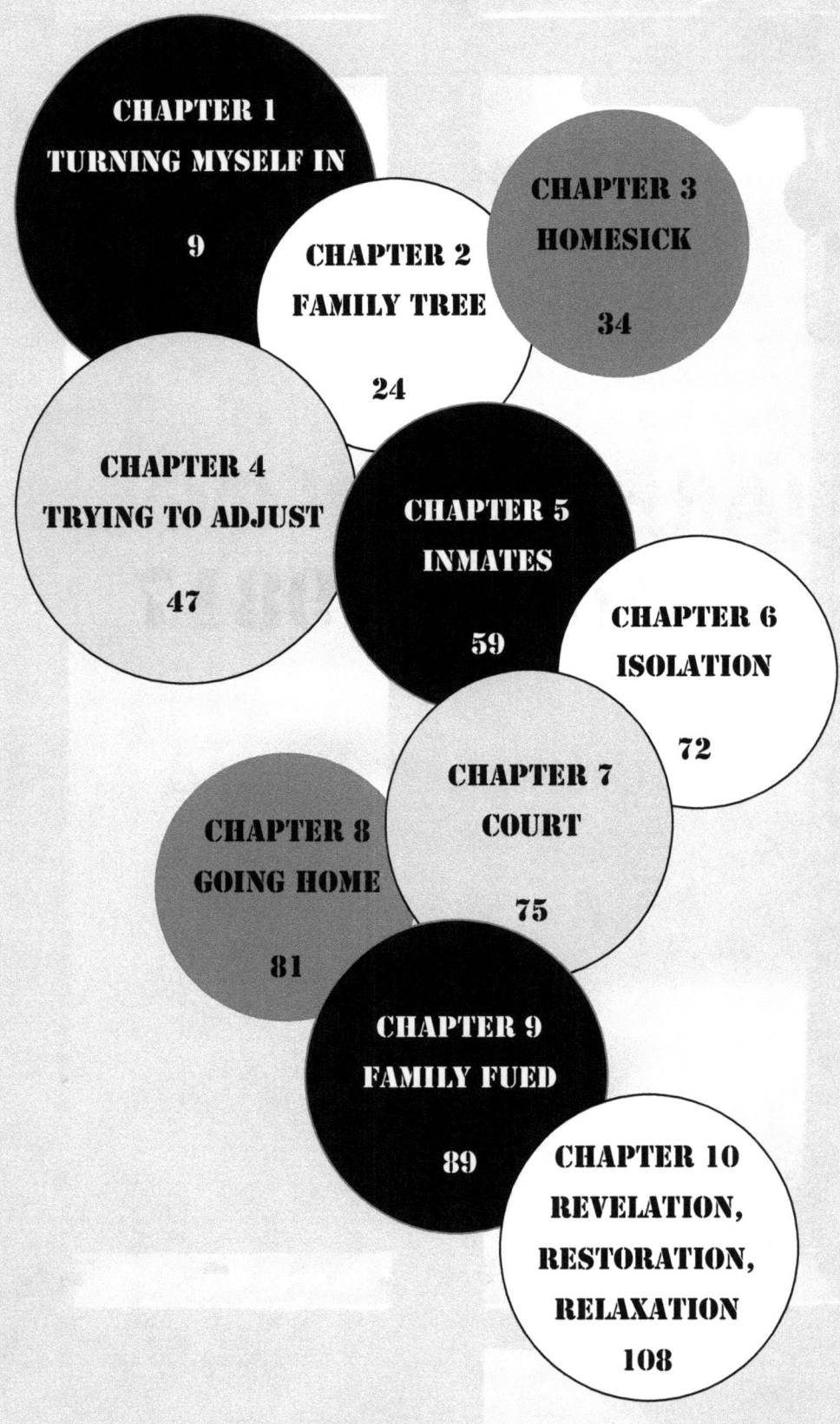

JAILED BY BLOOD: INMATE 798175

Turning Myself In

James 1:12

I guess blood ain't thicker than water, at least not in my family. That is according to my brother, Craig. I considered him to be my best friend and confidant. I never thought he would have done what he did...not to me.

May 15, 2007 is one of the most memorable days of my life, besides the birth of my children. It was the day I went to jail for a crime I didn't commit. I received a phone call to my Florida home from Detective Larimore of Georgia on May 14, 2007, stating that he received a complaint that I had unauthorized use of my dad's social security number to open up a few utility accounts back in 2005 when I lived in Georgia. His phone call was quite surprising as it was disturbing, especially when he said that he was putting a warrant out for my arrest. My heart just dropped to the bottom of my feet. At that moment, a thousand and one things went through my mind like what about my babies, the home I just obtained for them, what about my career? I didn't know what to do.

I was completely stunned, especially after he said the call he received was from my dad. Right then, I knew something wasn't right because my dad, at the time, was in Israel and had been there since 2003 with no plans of ever returning to the states. It cost way too much for him to do so, or even to call. I then knew that it had to be Craig.

For months, Craig has tried to get me to move to Florida in the same city as he, stating how nice the homes were and even emailed me a website link to look up the homes via a virtual tour of the interiors. I must admit that when I saw how beautiful the houses were, I was sold. The homes ranged from $200,000 to $500,000 to purchase and to rent, they ranged from $900 to $3000 per month. You would get more house for the money and beautiful stucco homes with tile roofs and high ceilings. I had to get one of those houses for my kids and I did just that July 7, 2006. I worked three jobs: the first job was at home on the Internet working in my career field as medical quality assurance auditor from 7AM to 3PM Monday through Friday, the second job was from 5PM to 10PM as a housekeeper in a hotel Monday through Friday, and the third job was delivering newspapers from 2AM to 6AM on the weekend. I saved for the move and added the child support I was getting from my ex-husband, Ryan, for the girls and from my ex-fiancé, Donovan, for the twins.

The kids and I packed up and Craig drove up from Florida to Georgia so we could follow him down for directions to our new home. I previously contacted a realtor and made transactions via fax of a lease agreement and the mailing of a money order for the first security deposit to hold the house. I had to make sure I had a roof over my kids' heads because Craig informed me that his wife, Tracey, did not allow any of Craig's family members to stay in their home. She also looked down at folks because they were not Jehovah Witnesses like they were. It took us about seven hours to get to our destination and when we finally did; we pulled up in the driveway of my new home where I met the realtor and her husband, who was the "handyman." When we got there, they took us inside and showed us a three-bedroom, two-bathroom home with a two-car garage that was approximately 1700 square feet. Since I already paid the first security deposit of $1000, it was now time to pay the rent of $925. I would not have this for a few days later when I would receive my direct deposit from one of my clients. Craig and I had already agreed that he would take care of it for me and I would pay him back a few days later.

As the kids and I were unpacking, setting up house, and settling in, Craig would come over daily with wine for he and I to drink and pizza, hot wings, and soda for the kids. We would talk and gossip like we always did when I was in Georgia, talking about how worse things have gotten between him and Tracey. From the way he talked about her, it was like he despised her, but I couldn't understand why he stayed in the marriage. I thought maybe it was because their religion didn't allow divorces. The whole thing was just strange to me and to add on more drama to their marriage, Craig's son hated Tracey and refused to call her "mom," and Craig would always refer to her as "that bitch." I asked him why not just remove himself from the situation? He never really would answer that question and I wouldn't push it, so I just listened to him vent to let out frustration and anger because he would be so upset to the point where it gave him migraines.

After a few weeks of getting settled into my new home, Craig informed me that he and Tracey were getting a divorce because he was "fed up" with her not contributing financially, as this was their third time being evicted by her hands. Tracey had her reasons of why she refused to contribute and gave a ludicrous statement of, "my momma didn't pay no bills, my daddy took care of everything, so I shouldn't have to pay no bills." Because of that very statement, they were always being evicted because he didn't make that much at his job to take care of the house for a family of five. Craig then asked if he and his son could stay with my kids and me because in his own words, "I'm through with that bitch." Of course I told him yes, he was my brother, my best friend and he had my nephew.

I added that they could stay until my lease was up and that he could even take his time to find a place that he really wanted for him and his son. I also told him that he didn't have to pay any bills, to just save his paychecks. Craig calculated that if he did that, he would save a total of $10,000 over a year's time. Now, since he was receiving food stamps for his son, I did tell him to buy the food and he agreed to it.

That Monday morning, we went to the middle school to inform them of our plans and to have his son's address changed to my address so he could catch the school bus with my 13-year-old daughter, as they went to the same middle school. We had already had a letter typed up and notarized of the change of address. The school registrar didn't have a problem with making the changes in their system until Craig mentioned that Tracey's 14-year-old son wished to leave his own mother and live with Craig at my house too. A red flag went up for me right then because he didn't mention this before. The school registrar stated that since Tracey's son was not Craig's biological son, he had to have permission from her in order to make such a change. Craig then gave the school registrar Tracey's work number and they contacted her and informed her of the changes that wished to be made and asked her to come down to the school at that moment to either give permission or not. Tracey worked for the school system in the transportation department, so it was nothing for her to get to us in a timely manner.

QUIET STORM

As she arrived, the school registrar went out into the hallway to greet her along with the principal and after they completed their discussion, they all returned back to the small office where Craig and I were patiently waiting. I couldn't help but to notice how Craig was in complete silence and seemed nervous with his one knee bouncing up and down and arms folded and his eyes looking every which way, except in my direction. When I called his name, he didn't even acknowledge it. The school registrar came in with a look on her face of surprise and stated that she was hearing an entirely different story than the old "divorcing my wife" story that Craig fed to both her and myself.

Tracey was right behind her and she looked directly at Craig and asked, "were you going to just leave me and Zaria, (her daughter), out in the cold?" He didn't answer. She asked again and still, no response. Then she turned to the school registrar and stated that they were all basically homeless, as they were being evicted from their home. The registrar then turned to me and asked if I had a problem with the entire family living in my home until they found a place to live. Shocked that she asked me, I looked at Craig, he still looking every which way, but my way, remained in silence with me still looking at him with a stare of "say something," but he didn't and the school registrar asked me again and I told her, "Uhh, no, I don't have a problem with it." What else could I say? I would look like a monster saying no after she just stated that her and her daughter had no place to go. I had to say yes.

I tried to make fun out of it and said, "we can all just have a good time together as a big family and eat pizza for dinner tonight," but no one thought it was funny...not even me. I was just upset because that was the second red flag. My own brother played me, but before I allowed myself to digest that discovery, I again gave him the benefit of the doubt, why...I don't know. I then added per the school registrar's request to add Tracey and both her children's names to the letter we originally wrote for Craig's son and they re-notarized it. As we were walking out the door, Craig was still silent and I noticed he lagged behind me and waited to walk with Tracey and I overheard her ask him, "Did you tell them that we were getting a divorce?" and he answered, "no, I guess they just assumed it." There it was...confirmation. The third red flag and strike and I was made a fool. Things have never been the same since then. It went from bad to worse. Tracey went back to work and Craig and I got in his car where he was dropping me off at home and he had to return back to work. I sat in silence trying to digest the vibe of being "happy" I sensed from him when he asked me if anything was wrong. I just couldn't believe it. Not this brother.

He and I were really close and I considered him to be my best friend and he played me like I meant nothing to him. It was no secret that our family was not close-knit, but I at least thought that he and I broke that chain. I was wrong. Why didn't he just say that they needed a place to live because they were being evicted? Why did he go through all the mess of lies and BS? It wasn't even necessary. When we got to my house, he came inside and was quick to speak and told my kids and his, whom were already at my house, as school had not yet started, that I invited Tracey to stay with us. I couldn't believe it. Trying to speak over the kids and his constant, "I can't believe she invited her," I couldn't get a word in edge-wise. I just surrendered my eyes and hands to the ceiling as I looked up and spoke to the Lord in silence and said, "Help me."

A few days went by and Craig was filling my garage up with their furniture very quickly. I had to rearrange my items that I had in the garage, including my pool table and old leather couches to accommodate their belongings. In the meantime, Craig was still professing that he and Tracey were getting a divorce and she was still "that bitch," when she wasn't around, but when she was, they got along just fine. They would text each other throughout the day. If she was in the garage, which she was often, and he was in the living room watching TV or if one of them were out at the store, they would text. When their family got together at night to watch TV in the living room, it was a barrel of laughs for them, as they thought Bart Simpson was so hilarious. He would cook dinner for everyone, but they all ate together. They all still went to church together; they didn't skip a beat on doing things that families do, even go to the park and the beach together.

When she wasn't around, he would pretend to be mad and always bring up that she was the reason for their eviction because all they "supposedly" needed to stay in their home was $175. The same $175 I offered to pay, but he refused to accept, stating that he wanted her to pay it, but it was too late and he found out after snooping in her safe deposit box, that she was actually sitting on $1500. He later found out that she received that money from an agency that provided funds and shelter to battered women. Before I moved to Florida, they had just gotten back together and she lifted a restraining order on him because she left him for abusing her. So, her reason to him for not using that money is because it was for her children, but she actually used most of that money hiring two different small moving van companies to move most of the items she had before marriage into a storage unit. Then he would complain that she would give him the "silent treatment." That drove him crazy, but I never noticed it from her to him, however, "that bitch" did give me the silent treatment. I tried to make conversation with her one afternoon when Craig conveniently disappeared, which he did often for several hours and would have his cell phone turned off...hmmm. I noticed Tracey sitting on the couch in the living room and I wasn't doing much of anything I was just about to shut down my medical work on the Internet and all the kids were outside, so I decided to pull myself away from the PC and talk to her. I was telling her, complaining about the chaise lounge piece of furniture that I was waiting on to be delivered, as it has been weeks past my due date to receive it and she cut me off in a snappy tone with, "I know what a chaise lounge is" she then got up and went to my garage and did not return. I was flabbergasted. I didn't understand her actions and started looking at her like the bitch she really was. Then I gave "that bitch" the benefit of the doubt and thought that maybe Craig's disappearance and being unreachable was bugging her or maybe she was just embarrassed and felt ashamed that she and her kids had to come live in my home, so I went back into my room and watched TV. After a few minutes, I heard the door from the kitchen that led to the garage open up and she came back out and commenced watching TV.

    I waited for at least 20 minutes and then came back out of my room. I tried to make conversation with her about the show she was watching as I sat on the other couch and she didn't look at me or speak a single word and got up and went back into the garage. I was done. Then when Craig finally showed his sneaky face, "the bitch" came out of the garage, after two hours and she was nonstop, couldn't shut her up running off at the mouth. I then joined in their conversation and "the bitch" actually responded to me then. What the hell? What was wrong with her?

After time, days and months went by, she just got bold with it and said to hell with it, I'm not speaking at all and she didn't, but only one time when I had to inform her about leaving dishes piled high in both sides of my sink overnight. The bitch spoke then and said, "Uh, um, well, I always do that so they can soak." Trifling self, I let her know that I don't do that EVER. NO dishes are to be in my sink after bedtime. One thing about me, I keep a clean house, you would have to with little ones and my youngest were 3-year-old twins at the time and my 3 older girls knew better. My mother always told me that the cleanest rooms in a woman's home should be the kitchen and bathroom. I don't know what "that bitch's" mom told her.

As time went by, they all got bold and slick at the mouth, including their kids. Craig and Tracey were bold in a way of actually having sex on my living room floor. One night, my daughter and I was watching TV in my bedroom and we heard a loud moan, we quickly opened my door and asked what was wrong, it got quiet then he spoke up and said, "oh, she was just laughing." I haven't even had relations in my own house out of respect for my children and myself. Then another time, my daughter called me on my cell phone and said there was an argument between Tracey's son and my 13-year-old daughter. When I'm not working, which is usually on the weekends, my kids like to listen to music on my computer.

My kids and I like all kinds of music, but one of our favorites are rap/hip hop music, R&B, but this was just horrible to Tracey and her kids ears so her son spoke up and requested to listen to "Cry Me A River" by Justin Timberlake. My 13-year-old, Nevaeh, refused him and he got mad and said to her, "your just like those ghetto girls, your the type that's going to end up with a baby" and commenced to commenting with his "flamboyant ways" that she had a "black girl body," which in his little mind consisted of a big butt and breasts. My eldest daughter, then 17-years-old, did everything to not haul off and bust this bougie little nigga in the mouth. Then my 18-year-old, Summer, went to inform the mother, but noticed that she was already listening and did and said nothing. After she told me, I told Craig, he and I were at Wal-Mart at the time. He said that he would talk to her and her son, of which he did, but it didn't make a difference. They still continued their ways.

Now at this time, I didn't have a car, so I worked two accounts, one in the morning for eight hours and one at night for eight hours to save up enough for a down payment at least, but before I could purchase a vehicle for the kids, Craig put down $1400 on a bigger car and traded his smaller one in and a week later, Tracey paid cash of $1800 on a van and traded her car in. After I saw this, I got pissed and told Craig that I needed money towards bills for them staying at my house. (Now I said he didn't have to pay any bills because then it was only supposed to be him and his son, but now was a different story with his entire family in my house).

He said it would be no problem, but that he knew that it would be a problem for her. She didn't want to give up any type of money, in Craig's own words, "that was just how she is." He gave me $100 and she gave me nothing. At this time, they had already stayed going on three months and just because Craig bought food, it didn't mean my kids and me had a chance to eat it, as they all ate as if it were their last meal.

When the boys came home from school, they went straight to the refrigerator and actually sat and ate a baloney sandwich, a hotdog, a bowl of cereal, and a few chips with cookies on a napkin, all in one setting and still ate three helpings of whatever dinner was for the evening. It was always three helpings. It was like they were stuffing themselves on purpose so we couldn't eat. I guess they figured since their dad was buying the food, they had a right to eat it, but they failed to realize they were in someone else's home, but they had no consideration and didn't care if it showed. My kids and I had to eat out and when we did buy snacks, we had to hide them in my bedroom closet inside of a box on top of my shelf or underneath my bed.

It was all taking a toll on my kids and I...just too much, they had to go. I did not want to make a scene in front of the kids and since Tracey never cared to indulge in any type of conversation with me, I sent her a text message and told her that they had to leave. I received no response from her, but instead got a call from Craig letting me know that Tracey forwarded my text message to him and he had the audacity to ask me to just wait until she gets a few more paychecks, then put her out. Now this came from a person that stated to me that he wanted nothing to do with her and planned on divorcing her, but here he was telling me, not asking mind you, to let her stay and get a few more paychecks. Little did he know, I meant for all of them to leave. I was not going to put this girl and her kids out by themselves even if "the bitch" was being rude to me, she was still a woman with children and since Craig set the whole thing up, I decided he needed to go with his family. After all, they seemed to get along just fine to me and he needed to be a man and take care of his family the right way. They stayed in my house for three long months and enough was enough, especially when my daughter told me about him putting eight large pieces of ice down my three-year-old son's diaper and thinking it was funny to watch him squirm and cry. He would also throw him up in the air and then pretend not to catch him until he hit close to the bottom, and when my son would walk, snatch his pants down. He aggravated him...cruel humor. I wondered why my son would run to me whenever Craig came into the house. I just kept my son up under me whenever Craig was around.

After they left, they found a house just that quick, but that didn't matter to Craig...it was on then. He had been trying to get revenge on me ever since, ignoring my text messages and voice messages to him that he and the kids could come by and visit us anytime, he never responded. He knew I was on probation from a forgery back in 2003 with Donovan, the twins' dad, that I so stupidly allowed him to convince me to do (love makes you do crazy things). I had only a year left to go and Craig was not going to let me complete that year in peace, so he tried everything he could to violate me. He went as far as to tell lies to authorities by calling my probation officers supervisor, telling him that my probation officer and I were having an affair, but the supervisor didn't believe him because of the great credibility the probation officer held with the office. Nonetheless, I was switched from that officer to a woman to avoid gossip in the office. Now since that didn't fly, he tried to put a temporary protection order out on me stating that I was constantly harassing him and his family.

We went to court and he complained of so many lies it was ridiculous and he sounded like a little wimp with this six foot, 200 pound, deep voice man that was supposedly "feared for his life" from me. It made him even madder when the judge told him that his courtroom was not the place for Craig's problem. All in all, the judge saw right through his lies and saw Craig for what he was, jealous and revengeful after I told my side of the story of the real reason why we were in court. I held no punches and brought printed copies of bad reviews Craig had placed, letting it be known that it was definitely him, on the Barnes and Noble website where books that I authored were advertised. Then I let the judge know about Craig's freeloading lying self with the whole story of how he and his family actually ended up in my house in the first place, which led me to ultimately ask them to leave, and how things really got ugly from Craig toward me when I moved into a replica of the home they were evicted from. This was not on purpose, as there were so many houses built the same way from the same builders. I needed the space, as my old house was a three-bedroom at 1700 square feet and the new place was a four-bedroom, two-bath of 2200 square feet. I told the judge that he was jealous because I was a single parent of five children, but was fortunate enough to make it on my own and they were a two-income family and couldn't make it together. I had no help from state welfare, only God and my business. Craig didn't like that one bit, along with being so angry because I wouldn't let him use me anymore. Needless to say, the judge dismissed the case. Craig was hot and steaming. The kids and I would often see him driving by their bus stop and by our house. He had to have been searching a while to actually find out exactly where we lived. So I put out a no trespass warning against him. That didn't stop him though. You see, back in 2005, when I lived in Georgia, I obtained a gas bill and phone bill in our dad's name.

  Our dad actually gave me permission in 2003 as a "gift" for not being there all my life just before he left the United States to move to Israel on a permanent basis. He even told it to my mom as well. That was our dad's way of helping me out financially because my credit was not that great since my divorce. I didn't utilize that permission until I actually needed the help, which was in 2005 and my other brother, Jason called the utility company and pretended to be our dad and established the bill at my residence for me. I had forgotten all about this because it was nothing to be concerned about, but Craig didn't forget about it and he made remarks on the Barnes and Noble review on one of my books that the "author was under investigation for identity fraud." I then began receiving instant messages from our other brother, Jason. Now, even though the siblings didn't talk much to each other, I had communication with a select few, there are eight of us, three boys and five girls and I talked to the boys on a regular basis and had brief contact with one of the sisters. Everyone was just spread out. Jason shocked me because he and his wife had just came to visit with me and the kids at the old house one month before all this began with Craig and now Jason and Craig was in cahoots and Jason stated that I was going to jail and how funny they thought that was. Jason and Craig usually did not speak. Craig didn't speak to anyone in our family except for me. One reason was his religion, the other reason was the two of them didn't get along, but they got along long enough to try and destroy my world. I tried to plead with the detective and begged him to believe me that my dad didn't make that phone call from Israel, but the detective was so nasty and so mean that he hung up on me. I called him back and he hung up again. I called him back and this time he listened as I told him that I was just going to turn myself in because I did not want to put my kids through anymore hurt that they were already going to endure. I did not want police coming to my home placing me under arrest in front of my children. I immediately called the prepaid legal program I had membership with and explained my situation. They gave me a number to a lawyer within the network in Georgia, which was the state that I was going to need a lawyer in. His name was Stan Ferguson with Bond and Ferguson Law Firm. When I spoke to him and explained the situation, he informed me that I was going to spend some time in jail, but only for two weeks and he would have me out on bond. I believed him and convinced myself that I was strong enough to deal with whatever came my way. I then placed confidence in him, as he ran down to me his credentials. I then placed it all in God's hands.

    Strange thing, I became at peace with where I had to reside for the next two weeks and I was not so afraid to go to jail. That didn't concern me, but me having to leave my children; that was the hurtful part. I sat the kids down and tried to find the right words to tell my children that their mother had to go to jail. What are the "right words" for something like that?

QUIET STORM

The lawyer had checked periodically and no warrant had been placed by the detective, so I had the rest of the day and night to prepare my children for what was about to take place and I took every second as if it were my last. Throughout their tears that never seemed to end, I stressed to them how important it was to keep our home and transportation. They were not to say anything to anyone, but to go with the flow. Summer and my eldest daughter already knew how to run my business in editing/proofreading documents ever since they were 13 and 15 years old. They were to split shifts and keep the accounts going smoothly in order to keep the income coming in to keep the roof over their heads. I showed them what utility bill was due on what date and left my bankcard that was connected to my checking account with them to pay the bills online, as I had all my utility accounts setup on the Internet. The whole time in explaining and preparing my children for this nightmare, I was dying inside and fought hard to not cry that a burning lump formed in my throat from holding back tears. I told them to continue doing their normal routines of going to school and church. Summer had already graduated high school, so she kept the twins. I told them to continue going to church on Sunday for service, Thursday for Bible study, and Friday for Youth Night. I kept trying to convince the kids that everything was going to be okay and instilled in them how important it was to stick together and take care of each other. We held a prayer chain together with holding hands in a circle, even the twins, and just prayed together, but it didn't stop their tears.

After several hours passed, they became confident in their prayers and eased up on the crying. The twins, of course, didn't understand what was about to happen, but they knew something was going on and they just remained silent, listened and stared at us. After praying, the older three said that they felt in their hearts that everything was going to be all right.

After they calmed down for a few, they watched TV and I had some time to myself and I went into my closet, my sanctuary, where I often prayed and dropped to my knees and broke down with tears that stemmed from mental exhaustion and disbelief. I begged God to give me the strength I needed to face the unknown and to give my children the strength they needed to keep going. My prayers and tears were interrupted with a phone call from my lawyer stating that the warrant had taken place that read it was a "warrant pending surrender" and it read that because I told the detective I was going to turn myself in. I then called my probation officer that was well aware of the situation and told her that the warrant had been filed. She couldn't see it because it was "pending surrender," and it was not posted nationally, but she gave me permission to leave the State of Florida.

I decided to turn myself in, because had I not, I would have been arrested, taken to Florida jail and made to wait for Georgia to expedite me, which could have taken anywhere from two weeks to a month and I didn't want to wait that long in jail staying away from my children. I wanted to get it over with and be back home in two weeks as promised. I remember hearing from somewhere that when you go to jail, you can't have extensions in your hair, so I had my kids take my extensions out and I wore it natural, then I went to the nail salon and had my acrylics removed. I remember when I was sitting there looking around at all the people while some spoke and some smiled, and here I was getting my nails removed so I can go to jail in a few hours while they were getting pretty just because.

After I returned home, I called on Mrs. Lisa, an older woman friend of ours that was there for Donovan and me when we got into trouble back in 2003. She told me to pack a suitcase and leave it at her house for when I got out so I could shower and put on fresh clothes. I did just that and called on an associate of mine named Marvin who had an airport shuttle business to give me a ride to the bus station. Before he arrived, my kids and I took our last moments together and filled it with a bunch of "I love you's," hugs, kisses, and tears. When Marvin arrived, I took my last hugs and kisses, and drove away from my children to go to a jail in Sparta, Georgia. I was going to take a bus there. I told Marvin what happened and as we talked, the more we began to piece things together.

There was something that the detective mentioned that didn't sound quite right, he said that my dad gave my brother Power of Attorney to press charges on me and that just couldn't be since that type of Power of Attorney does not exist. There is only financial Power of Attorney and to have Power of Attorney signed over to someone, you have to be present to sign the paperwork in the presence of a notary and my dad never came back to the states, in fact, it was impossible to get hold of him. The only communication we had with him was email. A game of an evil setup was definitely being played on me, but since I had already told the detective that I was turning myself in, I had to make good on my word. Marvin was reluctant to let me go, as he thought the whole thing was a BS game, so he made the decision to drive me to Georgia instead since it was only six hours away. He said that if it turned out that a game was being played, he could take me back home to my kids. I then called my kids and told them of my whereabouts and what I was going to do like check into a hotel to think about my situation and try to prepare myself mentally to actually be in jail. My girls setup a separate hotel room for Marvin and myself via my bankcard over the phone and all I had to do was show my ID when I got to the front desk, of which I did just that after we went to a restaurant to have dinner, my last real meal as I called it. We arrived at the hotel just a little after 11 p.m. that night and checked in two rooms down from each other. I talked to my mother and oldest brother that lived in Illinois and then spent the rest of the night talking to my kids. By this time, they were completely confident that I was coming right back home since I told them about the talk Marvin and I had and discovered the discrepancies and holes in the detective's phone call. They felt the same way, as my mother and brother had that a trick was being played on me from the hands of Craig and Jason.

Around 1 o'clock in the morning, I finally hung up with my children and I then received a text message from Donovan, completely oblivious of what was going on, telling me to cancel child support. I sent him a text message back telling him to get a job so they can garnish wages and to not bother me no more for the rest of the evening/morning. There was no way I could tell Donovan what was going on. For one, I didn't think he cared enough. Around 8 o'clock that morning, Marvin knocks on my door and stated that he was taking me back home to my kids because he thinks it was all a lie, but before I made that decision, I called my lawyer again and told him what I thought about the whole ordeal and he sounded as if I was speaking Chinese. He didn't know what I was talking about. All he knew was that there was a warrant with my name on it, waiting for me to turn myself in and according to him, I had better hurry up and get there. I told Marvin to go ahead and take me and while en route, I dropped off my suitcase at Mrs. Lisa's and headed out to the County Jail to turn myself in, of which I beat the warrant there.

    Here I was standing in front of a bunch of sheriffs trying to get inside their jail. I had to wait at least 30 minutes before the warrant showed up.

QUIET STORM

Family Tree

Ephesians 6:4

While I waited for the warrant to show up, I began to think about the real reason why I was there and I thought back to my siblings of how close we all were not.

My parents were married for 13 years with eight children, three boys and five girls. I was the youngest so I only heard about all the horror stories of abuse inflicted upon all of them, including my mother at the hands of our dad, Anthony. From what I heard, it was more than just the physical abuse; it was torture, rape, and cruel mental and emotional abuse. The oldest sister, Leslie, at the tender ages of five and seven, she was made to do dishes and our father stood beside her to make sure she cleaned the dishes correctly, but she must have done a dish wrong, according to him, and he just busted her in her skull with a plate that broke in half. Now back in those days, there were pretty thick plates and she still has the scar and knot on top of her head. Another incident occurred where he busted Leslie in the head again, but this time with his belt buckle because she couldn't get her math right or tell time correctly.

Every time he asked her what time it was, she tried to tell him, but she just didn't know and when she was trying to figure it out, "BANG!" was another hit, one after the other with the belt buckle. No one ever went to the emergency room because mother would always patch them up. Leslie still has problems with math and counts on her fingers and she's now 56. Then at the age of 12, she was wrist tied to the rails of the bed bucked naked and beaten by him with a belt soaked in water and not just a regular belt, but a belt five inches wide (back in the day, belts were wide, thick and real heavy leather). He beat her so bad that he beat the skin off her thighs and her back. Again, there was never any hospital visits and because mother was a nurse, she came home and would patch Leslie up and whomever he chose to abuse that day. They all were beaten in the same manner. His punishments were ridiculous whereas he made Leslie lay her face in another sibling's bedwetting. That same sibling that wet the bed, he made her drink her own pee for the accident. So many incidents occurred one after the other. It was crazy. I was told about an incident that happened where one of the middle sisters was also made to strip buck naked and beaten until she passed out for opening a box of donuts to eat from being starved by him, but just before her near death experience, he made the other siblings beat her as another punishment. Right along with physical abuse, there was constant rape to one of my sisters and mental abuse where he actually made Craig, who was four-years old at the time; eat his own feces straight out of his underwear. It was a punishment for having a bowel movement, which was an accident from being sick. My mother didn't have control, even though she was absent from working double shifts, however, she was not spared. He used to make her stand at the foot of the bed because she snored too loud for him.

He made her stand there until he went to sleep and if she tried to get back into bed, he would wake up and make her stand back at the foot of the bed with a fist until he was fully and completely asleep, that was the only way she was going to get back into that bed. Frustrated and upset the next morning, mother pushed over a fish tank that was in the house and when he heard the shatter from the tank hitting the floor, he ran into the room where she was and commenced to beating her as if she was a child being punished, but beating her his way with fists coming from a force behind eight inch biceps with over 20 years of red belt, 8th degree karate training. There were countless other beatings that have taken place from my dad to my mother and siblings. One incident that stunned me when told was when my mother came home from the hospital from having her tubes tied. I was eight days old.

She lied on the top half of the couch and laid me asleep at the bottom. He came home from work on a "lunch break" tripping off a drug called "acid", started talking gibberish and beat her so bad that she developed a hematoma in her stomach. He left right after beating her and left her bloody, left her for dead and there is no doubt in my mind that she would have died had not a home health nurse come to the door to perform her daily routine visit. Mother tried to motion for one of my sisters that was home from school that day to stay quiet, as she did not want the nurse to know that anyone was home, but the nurse was persistent and continued knocking and decided to peek through the inch curtain opened window.

Devastated at the bloody site, she saw that was my mother lying helpless on the couch, dying. The nurse motioned for my sister, five at the time, to open the door for her. She convinced her and as soon as the door was opened, the nurse called 911 and without knowledge of how mother got that way, called my dad, who had gone back to work and told him to get home as my mother was in bad shape. Never saying a word, he came home and actually helped mother into the ambulance. The very same person that beat her almost to her death. My mom ended up staying in the hospital for at least a week. What keeps running through my mind is that he actually left her for dead, as if bringing home diseases that nearly blinded Craig at the time she was carrying him, seven months pregnant was not enough. Praise God that Craig was not blinded, but it did make his hair fall out and it made him mentally slow that he later grew out of, but that incident like many others made my mother so fed up that she actually pulled a gun out on him and he used me as a shield to back out the door, get into his car, left me out on the sidewalk and pulled off.

Then there was another incident with a gun being pulled by my mother because my father was beating on her again and she grabbed hold of a gun and shot at him, but missed and when she missed, he snatched the gun from her hands and pistol whipped her in her head, drawing massive blood…all this in front of my siblings where mother cried out to our oldest brother to run and get our grandfather, but he was fearfully ordered to "stay put."

Until this day, mother has a slightly crooked smile and was diagnosed with Paget's disease, a disease where the bones break down more quickly, and when it grows again, it is softer than normal bones. There were so many hurting stories that were told to me by my mom and some of my siblings. He put such fright in my siblings that one evening all my siblings and mother were all having a good time in the kitchen laughing and talking until they heard the key to the door turn. At the same time, they all had to move their bowels from the fear of his very presence. Total silence when he entered the house, no more laughs or smiles. I just can't imagine what they all went through. There were incidents where it was always something like a battle for mother to get all my siblings to live with her on a permanent basis while going through their divorce, reasons being, my dad belonged to this high-powered organization where it included police officers, lawyers, and even judges. It was the type of thing where when my mother went to court to get my siblings back after being snatched by him, the judge wouldn't even see her, he would just ask, "is that Miss' so and so?" and the clerk would answer, "yes" and he would say, "I don't want to hear it" and the case would be dismissed, couldn't even call it a case.

Every time she would go to court, all my dad had to do was flash, in a very discreet way, a type of hand gesture sign of some sort to the judge and the case would be thrown out of court, so it became a battle between my parents with stealing my siblings back and forth. He would wait until they got off the school bus to get them.

Then childcare stepped in and asked the older siblings, which parent they wanted to live with. My siblings chose him because he bribed them with bikes and toys, but Daniel and Jason chose mother. Some time later, my mom received a call from childcare telling her that she needed to pick up my other siblings because my dad had beaten my sister Rachel until she passed out as I mentioned earlier and instead of him being placed behind bars, he was placed in a mental institution. (I think he needed to stay there). There were so many more horrible abusive stories, but all I knew about are recorded in this book in black and white and I believe it still haunts my siblings and mother til this very day. There was rumor that there was a curse on our family and sightings by evil spirits. Leslie told me of many different incidents that left me with my mouth hanging open. She was born with a veil over her face. We are not sure if that means anything, but we do know that she has premonitions and spirits seem to appear before her, but it is not in a way where she is fearful of them. She also has a gift where she can see the character of a person simply by a photo.

Not long ago, when two of my older sisters and I were reminiscing, they would recall their past and cry about their childhood, the beatings, and the scars. From what I was told, the oldest brother, Daniel, used to be beaten in the chest on a daily basis for whatever reasons our dad-felt necessary. I felt for a long time, he was afraid of him, even as a grown man with his own family, he still feared our dad, as I feel they all do, including my mother. Me on the other hand, I have no fear of him. I don't even like him nor do I respect him.

I tried to give him the benefit of the doubt even after hearing the terrible stories about him and decided to get to know my dad on my own and not go by what was told to me, so I reached out to him, tried to hold conversations with him, and reestablish a relationship, but it was impossible. He was every bit of the monster I heard about. He was naturally rude and arrogant.

From the stories of abuse I have been told, I believe there were a lot more abuse, but too painful for anyone to go in depth. There was also talk about sexual abuse and molestation from one older sibling to the other siblings, I was devastatingly tried, but spared...still brings tears to my eyes. Rumor had it that this sort of thing also occurred in my dad's family as well from him to his sisters. It all came out a few years ago. I didn't want to be anything like him. For years, I would hear my siblings blame my parents for the way their lives turned out by ways of our parents not being "wealthy" parents. Meanwhile, I don't know which sibling suffered the most, but the ones that I could remember were the oldest sister, Leslie. I had just gotten to know her when I was married with my three older girls at the time and lived in Virginia with my then husband, Ryan. She lived in Virginia for well over 10 years at that point in time and I decided to look her up. You see, I didn't know her very well after my parents' divorce, which was when I was about two-years old. The only thing I remembered about her when I was little was when Daniel brought Leslie to the house. I must have been about six or seven and I remembered thinking, "WOW!" I walked over to Daniel and whispered in his ear, "Is that your girlfriend?" I thought she was so pretty. He answered me and said, "No stupid, that's your sister." It's funny now, but not that funny then. She was my sister and I didn't even know her.

She has lived in Virginia for over 25 years now, on crack for 17 of those years on and off, conveniently supplied by an ex-boyfriend. I believe crack is an escape from her childhood experience of emotional and physical abuse and scars. Our other sisters, Tara and Rachel, used to be strung out on crack and heroin, of which I believe is from the past as well, a cry for help, a way out just like Leslie. Leslie has since been in rehab, is now married, and attending college to obtain a nursing degree in Williamsburg, Virginia. Rachel now lives in Mississippi, remarried with her children. Our other sister, Sara, who still lives in our home state of Pennsylvania, buried herself in the Holy Spirit.

    Tara, I can't even tell you where she is. The last I heard, she was residing in California somewhere, but that was over 10 years ago. I tried to find her and believe I did through a nationwide search company, but she sent the letter back I wrote her, as she didn't want to be bothered. She and I were never on bad terms, I believe it was her way of keeping the past buried by keeping the lines of communication closed with family members. Then later on in the years, I heard that she sent her daughter that she didn't get along with up home to Sara. I believe the child stayed there for not even a whole month before she ran away from Sara's home and now no one knows where she is. It hurts me, as I love all my nieces and nephews, but we are all so distant and there has been so much hurt throughout our family passed down to the kids, that nobody knows anybody and there is no hope for a family reunion...ever.

    As for my brothers, Daniel, he lives in Illinois, divorced with joint custody of his six-year old daughter. Jason, remarried for the fourth time, seven kids later, two in question, dodging child support enforcement, living in Arizona. Craig, now divorced from his wife, has one son and has a love child daughter while he was married to Tracey who lives up home in Pennsylvania. Craig still lives here in Florida. Jason and Craig were the two that seemed to inherit the bad traits of our dad with being a rolling stone, constant unfaithfulness, and abusing women. We heard Tracey and Craig in the garage one day arguing about the situation they were in with the eviction and she mentioned that things could be better between the two of them if Craig would stop putting his hands on her. He put his hands on her so often that she actually had to put a restraining order on him and moved her two children and herself out of their then home into a battered women's shelter. Craig would put his hands on her because of words once spoken from Tracey to her son about how she felt like she made a mistake in marrying him. Those words burned a hole in Craig's heart that he would bring it up on a constant basis. He even accused her of sleeping with her son because she confided in him so much.

QUIET STORM

She never talked much to Craig's son, as the two never got along, especially when she physically beat up the boy for yelling at her daughter. According to his son, she beat him up as if he was someone on the street. He was only 10 years old at the time. From what I knew of Jason and Craig, these two were exactly like our dad. They were mean to their women, didn't show much love to their children, and were so insecure and insincere. Jason was mean to his older child from his first marriage that he would abuse her something awful. He would make her clean the base boards of their apartment when she was little, around six-years old, with a toothbrush and if it wasn't cleaned to his liking, he beat her with his fists in her face, hit her in the stomach, and kick her with his boots in her side while she was down. She would have terrible bruises.

When she became a teenager, she ran away from home to her mother, but she was nothing but a prostitute and I mean that literally where she worked in a massage parlor that was nationwide busted for accepting money for sexual favors. So she ran away to our mother's house, where my mom did not want to return her. That caused a huge family feud, between Jason and our mom, but mother did what she felt was right, although it left a bitter taste in Jason's mouth, but his daughter didn't do right by living in mother's home. She was boy crazy, which resulted in her now having four babies, back-to-back with four different boys. She is now 19-years old, unemployed and a stripper. Jason has not been in her life throughout her new life experiences.

Jason failed his daughter just as his dad failed him and the rest of our siblings and as our dad failed our mother with being a husband, a provider, protector...a man. Our dad inflicted all this abuse for so many years on them and he has never been placed behind bars. I don't know what happened in our dad's childhood, but it couldn't have been all-good to treat his own blood family the way that he has and it wasn't just our family he mistreated.

After their divorce, he denied me and my brothers and sisters to get into the Army. At the age of 35, he then immediately married one of the women he was cheating on my mother with and had three children with her. As far as I know, he didn't beat them the way my siblings were beaten, but he must have done something awful to this white woman he married to make her cheat and get pregnant by another black man while they were married. From what I heard about her, after my parents were divorced and my siblings were young, almost teenagers, she would refer to them as "niggers" whenever it was time for them to come downstairs to eat after being made to wait until their kids were finished eating first. They informed our dad of such harsh mistreatment by his wife, but he didn't do anything about it. My siblings were lucky to even be fed according to them, as they were often starved.

In the meantime, my mom, Daniel, and my children were trying to reach my dad regarding what was going on and when they finally made contact, I got a call from my oldest daughter stating that my dad made it quite clear that he did not care and used those words exactly and even added that he didn't think I was his child. Wow, what a blow to me, not so much of the words, as I don't expect anything less from him, but it was a blow as far as my current circumstances. Here I was about to have my freedom taken away, leaving my children alone in another state and he puts the icing on the cake with stating that he didn't think I was even his kid. What a bastard!

Of course, I was his child, I believe he felt like that about me because when I did give him a chance to come into my life after I was married with children, I had to set him straight on bad mouthing my mom. He didn't like that I told him, "that if he couldn't talk to me about me and what was going on in my life, then he didn't need to talk to me at all." That was disrespectful to him, but not to me. I even said it nicely. I never judged him from what was told to me, I took the time and tried to get to know him on my own, but he turned out to be every bit of what was told and more in my eyes because his character was messed up. He has no personality. He is just plain mean, ignorant, and arrogant. He shows no respect to anyone. I remember when Craig was placed in jail for at least five years for what was classified as rape and he was then labeled as a pedophile. At the time, Craig was 17 and his girlfriend was 15. He never raped her, but her family was bougie-type black folk with a little bit of money and they didn't quite exactly see Craig as the "ideal boyfriend" for their daughter, but he didn't care what they thought. He even ran away from home to New Jersey where she lived.

We lived in Pennsylvania at the time and she was visiting our neighbors, which were her cousins. Craig and the girl hid their relationship from her parents, but one day, while her parents were at work, they were in her house alone, but someone came home early and they were busted. The girl hollered rape and the cops were called and they put him in jail. My mother tried all she could to help him and Craig clearly didn't want her to help, in his own words, "your going to mess stuff up and make her parents mad" so my dad was called and he was no help at all. He sent word to Craig to be careful not to get "raped." Craig spent five years of his life in prison and during that time, I felt like apart of me was missing. We would write each other back and forth. Craig loved music so much that he would have me send him lyrics to some of his favorite songs. One song in particular to help him get over the girl was called "All Cried Out" by Lisa Lisa and the Cult Jam. Even after all that and being in jail, he still had the girl in his system. In one of his letters he told me about a six-foot, 300 pound white guy that he had to share a cell with that "tried him" and Craig put a karate move on the guy's knees with a swift kick that brought him down. Needless to say, he didn't have anymore problems out of the guy. While in prison, Craig utilized his time getting himself several certificates in learning computers and different types of software.

What got him out of prison was a letter from the girl stating that she was sorry she lied about him raping her, however, the authorities still kept him under Megan's Law and everywhere he went, he had to register as being a sex offender.

He was given 10 years of parole. I was just happy that he was getting out of prison. It was an awful feeling to know he was sent to prison for something he didn't do. Then once Craig was out for awhile, there was another incident with a crack head that hollered rape, but I don't quite know the outcome of that one, but he did go back to prison for it. Now this crime, he did do. As time went by, Daniel told him about how to let parole run out, so he registered his address to another state. After his parole ran out at a fake address, he no longer had to register as a pedophile, which was just recently done.

Still waiting for them to find the warrant on me, I watched people coming in to visit others that were in jail. A young lady asked me which pod I was going to, as she assumed I was there for visiting, but I didn't know what she was talking about. I didn't know what a pod was. I just told her that I wasn't going to a pod. She just looked at me as if to say what was I doing there. Then they called my name. They found the warrant. Detective Larimore didn't have the warrant nationwide; he wasn't going to do that unless I didn't show up. A female sheriff came out to take me to the back. She looked really mean. I didn't say a word to her, but she spoke to me to ask what was I in there for and I told her because I got a gas bill in my dad's name and my brother called Georgia police and pretended to be my dad and said he wanted to press charges, but it was actually my brother who called to obtain the bills in my dad's name.

Her look at me changed from evilness to "that's a damn shame," which is exactly the words she spoke after I told her. She said, "Your own family did something like this, makes no sense." She was right and I was embarrassed. Then my embarrassment dropped to humiliation as she had to run her fingers through my hair to ensure I had no contraband, then I had to give her my shoe laces, open my mouth, lift my tongue, and she searched me where she groped me firmly on my breast and in between my legs. It was awful. I didn't feel much like a woman anymore. I belonged to the state of Georgia. I was an inmate, a number, and a victim of circumstance.

QUIET STORM

Homesick

John 16:22

  After being touched in an uncompromised way, I was told to sit down on a bench until booking called my name to be fingerprinted and have my picture taken. I sat there and started looking at all the people coming in and going out. One young lady was brought in by a police officer without handcuffs because she was in pain and bloody. From hearing her story as she was talking to another soon-to-be inmate, the young lady was in a fistfight with her sister and a terrible one at that. The girls' forehead was busted open with blood trickling down the side of her face, her fingers and wrist was bandaged with blood seeping through, she had a gash on her shoulder blade where her shirt was half torn off. She stated the cop arrested her for them fighting in front of their small children, but she was just in a fistfight with her boyfriend just before she got into it with her sister where the boyfriend sliced her on the side of her cheek and the cop didn't arrest him, but took her instead. I immediately thought about my kids and I wanted so badly to wake up from this nightmare.

  Then my thoughts were interrupted with inmates dressed in blue uniform and chained from the waist to their wrists inside of a holding cell arguing, cussing each other out, calling each other all kinds of bitches and ho's. They looked so rough, so unladylike in appearance as far as their faces, as well as unladylike verbally. I immediately began to pray and ask God to please get me home as soon as possible. Even when the white women talked mess to the black girls, they bucked on them. No one backed down from no one. Moments later, my name was called to the counter by a female sheriff asking me health questions, if I was allergic to anything, pregnant, etc. After I finished with her, I sat back on the bench for only a few seconds before my name was called again to the back by a male sheriff to get fingerprinted and have my mug shot taken. This male sheriff had a sense of humor, but I didn't feel much like laughing and he vowed to make me laugh before I left his area. He asked me why I was there and I told him the same as I told the female sheriff that groped me and he said "oh, so your brother wanna tell shit, huh?" That made me laugh because I did not know this man and he was comfortable with his choice of words to me. He looked at me with a smile of "I told you so," he made me laugh.

As I was fingerprinted and had my picture taken, I could see on the other side of the door where the male inmates were being held and they were looking through the door window trying to get a look at any woman they could. One male inmate had the nerve to wink his eye at me. I gave him the most evil look I could make on my face and rolled my eyes hard at him, but it didn't seem to faze him one bit. He did not look away. I could still feel his crazy eyes on me. I didn't look his way again. Another sheriff came in and talked to the sheriff that was fingerprinting me and said that he had to take a wheelchair over to the male pod. When asked why, he replied with: "for some crippled fucker" and they started laughing and so did I. The one that was fingerprinting me, looked at me and said, "she think we crazy." I stopped laughing and had a plain look on my face and thought to myself, I bet they talk about all of the inmates like this and look down at them. Just being in there made me feel like nothing.

They didn't know who I was. They didn't know I was a child of God. They didn't know I had beautiful children at home waiting and crying for me. They didn't know I had my own business and that I was an author, trying to complete a book for cancer survivors. I was just another inmate to them, a number, and after he made my wristband and placed it on me, I was assigned a number, 798175. I was officially an inmate of the county jail.

I had to go out the door and sit back on the bench until a mannish female sheriff, as most of the women sheriff's looked mannish, walked mannish, and had deep voices, came to "dress me out" as they called it. When she did come to "dress me out," I had to give them my clothes and shoes, undress in front of her down to bra and underwear where they had to be taken away as well.

She saw the look of humiliation and embarrassment on my face and said to me, "I know, everyone has to do it." I cannot tell you how that made me feel. I had to change into their inmate blues and get the waist and wrist cuffs attached to me. Sitting there with the cuffs on, the further away from home I felt. I started thinking about my kids, my home, and my life. I began looking at all the other women sitting in the holding cells wondering if they had any children and how their children felt about their mom being in jail. Some of the women and many young girls talked as if they were back for the third and fourth times around. It was like they were used to it, like it didn't bother them at all that they were in jail. It seemed like they all knew each other too. This was nothing I wanted to get used to. It was humiliating and degrading. Your character wasn't looked at, just the fact that you were there, they treated everyone the same, like you were a criminal. For the ones that spoke as if it were just a "thang" probably deserved to be there, but I was different…wasn't I?

At least I thought I was, but they made me feel like I wasn't real quick. Being in jail was awful and I didn't even make it upstairs yet to get assigned a bed. Just hearing how these women talked to each other was enough for me. The atmosphere was cold and stale and the place was filthy. As time went by, I saw so many women being brought in by police officers, both young and old with an age range of 17 to 60 of all races.

Then the "trustees," that is what was printed on their white T-shirts, rolled a food cart over to the center of the floor accompanied by a sheriff and handed out what they called lunch. The lunch consisted of a small carton of fruit juice, a small bag of potato chips, a small round oatmeal cream cookie, and two sandwiches smashed together with salami and cheese inside and it didn't smell too good either. That "lunch" made me feel even more humiliated. I felt like crying. The sheriff uncuffed our hands so we could eat, but they could have left mine cuffed. In my mind, I was like, "what the hell is this?" I seriously wanted to cry. One of the inmates that was sitting next to me said out loud, not looking at me, but obviously talking to me saying, "if you plan on being here for a while, I suggest you eat now because dinner is not until 8 o'clock" and at this time, it wasn't quite 12 in the afternoon. I gave her my sandwiches and I ate the chips and cookie and took a few sips of the juice. I didn't want to eat too much nor drink a lot because I didn't want to have to use their bathroom…if you want to call it that. The silver-bowled toilet was out in the open. So, at this time, I didn't really have an appetite, but I forced myself to eat the little I did eat.

She was right. We sat there for all those hours until shift change, which was around 6 o'clock in the evening. The sheriffs were coming and going. At the end of the shift change, we were put inside of a holding cell, which was worse. It was one long cold bench with a toilet behind a half sized brick wall and one phone on the wall that was hogged by an inmate calling everybody under the sun, not using courtesy at all. Myself and three other ladies sat inside that cell for an hour or so until a sheriff took us upstairs. It was like going through a maze of their long cold brick hallways that I'm sure had stories to tell if walls could talk with metal doors, then an elevator where when you got in, inmates had to keep their back turned away from the sheriffs as if in shame and face a camera mounted on the ceiling of the elevator. Talk about more humiliation on top of more humiliation. The devil kept trying to creep into my thoughts and take over my emotions and make me hate my brother for what he did, but I continued to pray and asked God for strength, then I kept repeating to myself, "get behind me Satan." When we got off the elevator the sheriff led us down another long cold brick hallway with stories embedded within its walls, down into what was called an "R-pod."

Now I know what that young lady was talking about when she asked me what pod I was going to. That sheriff left us in the hands of another female sheriff and she uncuffed our wrists and took the chains from our waists. She told us each to take a pad, which was the length and width of a sleeping bag and just as thin.

We then was given a blanket that was wrapped up with a very thin bar of soap, a plastic cup with a toothbrush that was the size of a thumb wrapped in plastic and a clear small tube filled with a clear thick fluid that was supposed to be toothpaste, four maxi pads, two rolls of toilet paper, four pairs of underwear that some were stained in the crotch and butt, a few sports bras that were a dingy white, a gray sweatshirt with county jail lettering on the back of it, as did all the clothes, a few blue short sleeved shirts and pants and far from white sweat socks. Our shoes were like a burgundy colored plastic sandal with the name, "Bob Barker" imprinted on the sides of them. We were to keep all this wrapped up inside the blanket, sheet and pillow case and drag the bed pad into another locked door that only opened by a button operated by another sheriff inside a tower that was in the middle of the building with what they call dorms. There were six of these dorms that held up to 50 to 60 women.

When we walked in, it was like something off a movie with catcalls and yelling from these women of "fresh meat" or "new fish." I tried not to surrender my total mental status and place myself completely in the environment I was forced to reside. I had to keep my sanity. I was just non-stop praying for God to "keep me strong." Weird thing was, I was ready to cry like a baby about the awful food served, but when it came to being amongst these women and really being in jail, I was stone-faced and didn't feel like crying at all. God answers prayers. He gave me strength where I needed it the most and at the time...I needed it the most. Who says He isn't an on-time God. I wasn't scared or intimidated. I buckled myself down mentally and emotionally and made myself ready to deal with whatever and whoever came my way. I couldn't think about my kids anymore, they were my weakness. I had to cut them completely out of my thought process and prepare myself for the unknown, as I was now officially in the lion's den.

There were two levels with bunk beds the size of the bed pads that were the width and length of a sleeping bag. The bunk beds were made of metal with rust in most parts and the dorm was made up of women of all races. There were women everywhere, sitting at the metal tables that had metal stools attached either playing spades or scrabble, just sitting and talking or reading a newspaper. I went to the top tier and found a middle top bunk. I had no idea what to do with anything. I kind of stood there for a minute and digested the moment with thoughts of "oh boy." I must have looked confused because two females started to help me make up the bed with the sheet and blanket and showed me where I was to put the accessories given like the soap, toilet paper, etc. it was to be placed in a "cubby" that was underneath the bottom bunk where one side that was empty was mine and the other side was what they called my "bunkie." After I thanked them, they went back to their beds, which were across from mines. There were three sets of bunk beds on one side and four sets of bunk beds on the other side. This was called a "cut." Each cut had a total of seven bunk beds and there were two cuts upstairs and two cuts downstairs.

If there were no more beds, they made women sleep in what they called a "boat." It was a tad bit wider than the bed pads, but it was a plastic sized bed that you slept in on the floor. After I placed all my accessories inside my cubby, I sat on the steps and kind of glared at my surroundings when a woman looked up at me from the downstairs table who was looking at a newspaper with another woman and said, "You can come down here and talk to me, we all going through the same thing." I gave her a half smile and said "Nah, I'm alright" and I then got up from the steps and walked around the cut on the other side then something caught my eye...the bathroom and shower. The toilets were out in the open, no privacy whatsoever. There were three metal toilets that looked like the one downstairs in the holding cell that had a half of a brick wall to cover your goodies and a shower caked with mold and mildew that had 3 heads, but only one worked and the shower curtain was next to none. To be completely covered for privacy while taking a shower, you had to use your sheet or blanket. More humiliation.

I decided I have seen enough. I went back to my side of the cut and was headed for the bed until I was approached by one of the female inmates that helped me make my bed. She asked me what I was in there for and I told her the reason.

She and others that overheard me stared at me in disbelief and one of them spoke saying, "I can't believe they locked you up for that shit." Another one spoke and said, "They actually lock you up for shit like that, I got a cable bill in my cousin's name." I was starting to feel embarrassed at this time, even more so when I told them that I turned myself in. They were laughing and said they never would have turned themselves in. I explained that I had children and did not want the police coming to my home scaring or upsetting them. I did not want to sit in a Florida jail waiting for Georgia to take their time expediting me because who knew how long that would have taken. I then asked what they were in there for and the one responded with grand larceny, forgery, and theft by taking, but she stated that she didn't do it. Someone else was responsible, but that someone else signed an affidavit testifying against her. I didn't know what to believe about her not doing it, and I wasn't going to judge anyone, so I just kept an open mind and listened and talked to her about it, as she was clearly upset. One girl who was 19 was placed in jail for murder. I didn't even bother to ask, but from listening to her conversation, she was at a murder scene and fled, it wasn't clear if she did it or not. Then another spoke and said that she was arrested for shoplifting, but that she didn't do it. It was actually her younger brother who was stealing video games from a major grocery store, but since she was with him, she was charged as well.

She was only 17 and had been incarcerated for three weeks at that time, pregnant and waiting on a court date. She was a child around my kids' ages. I couldn't imagine any of my kids in this girl's predicament. That depressed me. She was put in jail for being with someone that was stealing. When she used her cell phone to call her mother to tell on her little brother, security caught them and they placed her little brother in a juvenile detention center and put her in jail. What a mess. I then asked them if they had any paper so I could write, as I had already had a pen that I kept in my pocket from downstairs in the holding cell. Writing was an escape for me and I desperately needed a quick fix. I went over to my bed (I hated saying that, "my bed" I never wanted to own anything in that place simply by saying it). I climbed onto the top bunk and began to write. I started off with thoughts and quotes of mine. Then ventured off into why not make another book. I always wanted to write about female inmates, now was the perfect opportunity. The more I thought about it, the better it sounded to me and then I could write about my own experience first, and then introduce the women. While I was pondering over what to name the book, I got down from the bunk and started walking around the dorm again in deep thought when it was interrupted with a call from the loud speaker stating that I had "first appearance." This was done in the downstairs part of the jail and your amongst women, as well as men inmates that all sat in the same room with men on one side and the women on the other and you listen to a judge on a television set that can see you and hear you.

She will call your case and name one by one, they usually did the men first and run their charges off to them and ask if they understood their charges. One guy had charges of armed robbery at a bank, doing drugs, selling drugs and he was offered a bond of $2000 and then asked if he can afford the bond and he said "no" and the bond was actually reduced to $1000 and of that he only required to pay 12%. All those serious charges and he was let out on bond. Unbelievable and here I was with a damn gas bill in my own dad's name and I was denied a bond. After first appearance was over, they took the men back and we followed shortly after.

I was upset. We were taken back upstairs, uncuffed, and let back into the dorm just after doing a quick head count of who all went. I began thinking about what just happened in first appearance, trying to digest it all when a sheriff that came into the dorm interrupted me and asked if she could talk to me for a minute. I didn't speak to her, I just walked towards her. She was concerned so she says of my silence and the look I had on my face of being upset. She stated to me that there was someone I could talk to as far as a psychologist if I felt suicidal or had thoughts of such. I laughed at her and told her that I was good, just new to this and walked away. She made me mad. Who in the hell did she think she was approaching me with an assumption like that. I climbed up on the top bunk and started writing short notes about what I had just experienced in first appearance, my surroundings, and what I heard through conversations amongst others.

Apparently, there were a lot of lesbians; nicknames "gayfers" in this jail and you would be able to recognize them. They either wore sagging clothes, like a dudes pants, or they would wear this multicolored handmade string made out of the thread of the inmate clothing, woven together and tied around their ankles. If it was worn on the left, then you are gay. They talked about their current relationships and past relationships with other women. They talked about it as if it were a relationship between a man and a woman. I was shocked, but kept writing. They talked about how they had sexual relations with another woman, and then they talked about their reasons for being incarcerated that pertained to drugs. Everyone that spoke about doing drugs talked about crack. They were not ashamed to talk about how they smoked it, what they did to get it, prostitution. It was awful. I can remember thinking to myself, "oh my gosh!" It was wild. When nighttime came, I didn't want to go to sleep around all these strangers. I stayed up at night and slept during the day to try to sleep my days away. I thought it would make the day go faster since the night went pretty quickly and 5 a.m. was wake up call for head count. It seemed like after midnight hit, the hours flew by. I just stayed up and read the Bible and started writing bits and pieces of this book. At 5 o'clock in the morning, you would hear an announcement from one of the guards in the tower to get up for head count. They performed a head count twice a day, one at 5 a.m. and sometimes between 4:30 and 5 p.m. It started to get annoying. I thought it was stupid because there was no way for anyone to escape.

There was a heavily locked security door to the dorm that could only be opened by the guard in the tower. So in between 5 a.m. and 5 p.m., no one had a way out and when they had "yard call" there was still no way to escape out there either, as it was a small, about the size of a regular living room with brick walls the height of a 2.5 story building with a cage over top. It was a tease, but inmates would race to get that little bit of outside air. I didn't dig it too much. I stayed inside and wrote or took a shower, which with most of the dorm outside, that gave me the perfect opportunity to shower and go to the bathroom. I wasn't comfortable showering or going to the bathroom with a full house, so to speak. With the shower and toilets being out in the open, I would wait until everyone went to sleep or go outside to use the toilet. I would hold myself for quite some time. Most of the women didn't care about taking a shower or going to the bathroom in front of each other. They would sit on the toilets and hold conversations. Nothing I wanted to get used to. I was so uncomfortable there; I actually slept with the flip-flop "Bob Barkers" on my feet that I got blisters that made it sore to walk with huge peels at the bottom. I also would never change into their provided long night T-shirt. I just slept in the clothes. I felt like wearing a nightgown and taking off those flip-flops was getting too comfortable so I refused. Besides, I only had two weeks, or so I thought.

The night before your court day, they announce through the tower that it is now 3 a.m. and you have 15 minutes to get ready. After you get yourself together, you ring the buzzer next to the speaker on the wall and let the guard know that your ready, they unlock the security door through the tower and guide you to another part of the jail about four feet from the dorm where you're amongst other inmates that have court on that day as well. Sometimes 15 to 20 women at a time sit and wait for a guard to come and put those blinging chains around your waist and wrists and if someone had a violent crime, they got an extra bling around their ankles. There was a young girl that had that extra ankle chain, and was barely 19, who got caught with guns for a second time. *Can you imagine that?* The guards then guided us in two lines of women chained together mastering a walk in unison down that long hall, into that camera watching elevator, then unchained to be placed in front of a scanner that scanned your whole body for contraband, then down to intake where you were placed in a holding cell til 7 a.m. Why they got you up so early, I will never know. I don't think anyone knows. You're sitting there in a cold closed up cell with one long bench, others sitting on the floor with one toilet, smelling each other's breath, listening to their stories of why they were there, and at times, listening to gospel singing and prayers to be able to go home after seeing the judge.

Around 6 a.m., they bring you breakfast in one of those Styrofoam trays that consisted of cereal, a small carton of milk that would not always be fresh/up-to-date, a piece of mystery meat that looked half cooked with red showing rawness, and a sometimes burnt muffin with fruit that wouldn't always be fresh. I gave my food away all the time. I heard someone say, "blend in or bond out." I wish I could bond out.

Even when it would be time for dinner, I would give my food away. They thought I was crazy. I thought they were crazy to be so happy to eat it. You would have to stand in a line, deal with people cutting in line and you give your name to the guard, who would mark you off on their chart. I felt like crying all the time when it came time to eat their food. I felt humiliated. I would hold back my tears. It was a routine for me. Stand in line, give my name, get the food, give it away, go to the bunk, put my head under the covers and cry silently and stay there until everyone went to sleep, get up at night, read the Bible and write my book. Inside those Styrofoam trays you would get a small square packet of what they called "kool-offs" instead of kool-aid and you would get a small blue packet of coffee. They called these "blue packs" and they were quite popular because they would "pop" the blue pack of coffee by pouring the dry grinded coffee onto their tongues chased with fruit punch, and sometimes they would mix the coffee in old cleaned out shampoo bottles, used as water bottles. You could get almost anything

QUIET STORM

for a "blue pack." They traded and auctioned off other foods for a "blue pack" like "cereal for a blue pack" or "blue pack for chips." It was like a whole other world.

When 7 a.m. came around, you would then be called out one by one, chained back up, and called by name to take a head count for whichever court you had to be in, either Superior Court or State Court. I was Superior because my charge was a felony. It was divided into those two groups and depending on what group you were in, you had to ride either in the long bus that was covered up on the inside with cages over the windows or you had to ride in a small closed up wagon with barely enough air to breathe and taken on a bumpy ride downtown to the courthouse. Some would try to sit by the small back window if it wasn't covered just to get a look at the outside while riding, which at times would be covered. Once you got downtown, there were a bunch of sheriffs that seemed to be meaner than the ones from where you came from.

When we got off the bus and patty wagon, we had to walk single file into the back door of the courthouse of what looked like a basement that led into a cell that looked so old and isolated and it was very cold. I was leading the front line and apparently the guard called out twice for me to stop walking. I didn't hear him at all, my mind was somewhere else. He finally yelled along with a female guard and came up to me and said, "What's wrong with you, you deaf or something? The female guard laughed and then he said, "Maybe you don't understand English" and he began to pretend to speak in Spanish gibberish and said, "Can you understand that?" I kept silent, looking straight ahead. We were made to stand up against the wall with arms and legs spread to be searched then we would go into the cell and make room for one another. If you didn't squeeze yourself on one of those two cold benches you would either sit on the floor or stand up and some of the women that knew each other laid their heads on each other's lap or sit on each other's lap. Sometimes, we sat down there for an hour, sometimes two hours before a sheriff would call your name in time for your court appearance.

Then you're led to another cell that was called the infirmary and it was even colder in there, just a little bit bigger cell with three bunk beds, a filthy tub and toilet. Across from that cell was where they kept the men, but you couldn't see each other, only hear each other and the inmates would talk to the men and the men were more than happy to talk back. I just occupied myself with my thoughts of prayer in being able to go home. For some women, they would end up having a "dry run," which meant they would go through all this nonsense to be there, but they would never see a judge. Their case would never be called, they were just put on the docket or their lawyer or public defender didn't show up, which often happened. Then they were taken back to the county jail. For the ones that were going to see a judge that day, we had to sit and wait until it was our court time. My court time always seemed to be around 1:30 p.m., so I had to wait a bit with dozing off in a chair. A sheriff would bring you lunch around 11 a.m. that consisted of peanut butter and jelly in packets with four pieces of smooched wheat bread, a bag of small chips, an oatmeal cookie, and a small carton of punch. Like usual, I would only eat the cookie, chips and drink and I had to be starving to do that. In between waiting for my 1:30 p.m. court appearance to take place, others were coming back from their 8:30 am and 9:00 am court appearances.

Only a few would have smiles because they were going home and the others didn't want to talk, which pretty much meant they weren't going home and may have had more time added.

My time came around and a sheriff came down to get me and a few others that had court at the same time. While going through their process of being chained back up and facing the wall of the elevator, I was psyching myself up to believing that I was going home. I could remember thinking this is my first and last time having to go through this mess. I can't wait to get home to my kids. Get back to my life. After we got off the elevator, they took us to a very small room that was hot and we were still chained up.

The room was next to a door that led to the courtroom and there was another door where the men were waiting to be seen as well. They would holler through the door trying to talk to any female inmate that would answer, but no one did, at least not on this day. Standing in that hot room for at least 30 minutes, a sheriff came to get me to see my lawyer. He looked like he didn't have good news. I just looked at him and said, "What?" and he said that Detective Larimore went on vacation for two weeks, which meant I had to stay in jail for another two weeks until we got a court date. Then since I was not violated from my probation from 2003, the judge violated me, which now made me a VOP, violation of probation and that usually carried a mandatory straight three months unless you had a damn good lawyer, and to add more salt to the wound, my dad added on two of his cellphone bills that added up to at least $600.

I told my lawyer that I didn't even know what those bills were and his words to me were, "either you pay it or stay in jail."

Talk about being crushed. I wanted to die. I wanted to ball up in a corner and cry like a little baby. I was so devastated. I knew that Detective Larimore was full of shit. He knew we had a court date today and he suddenly decides to go on vacation. I believe the bastard was trying to find more evidence, of which there were none. How could I tell my kids that I wasn't coming home as planned? They were going to be just as crushed as I was. At that moment, I felt like I was never going to be able to go home again. I was dying inside...I was homesick.

JAILED BY BLOOD: INMATE 798175

Trying To Adjust

Romans 12:2

After what felt like a fatal blow to my heart, the sheriff guided others and me back down to the cold cell in the basement. We had to wait another 3 hours until the bus and patty wagon came to pick us up to take us back to the county jail. I was in dead silence. If someone had spoken anything to me, I would have started crying and I didn't want to appear "soft" in there. I just kept my mouth shut, kept a mean mug look on my face, and held back my tears. After we got back to the county jail, we had to sit down in the holding cell of what they call "intake" for at least an hour before a sheriff came to take us back up to the dorm just before being searched again, this time with a machine that can see through our clothes, looking for objects. After getting back to the pod, a few others and myself were let back into our assigned dorms. They were bum rushed with questions of "what happened?" and "are you going home?" I think only one lady was going home from that morning. When someone is going home, the other inmates are genuinely happy for those individuals.

Everyone gets in their hugs and wishes them luck, then they swarm them with phone numbers of friends and relatives, boyfriends/girlfriends to give to them with a message to make calls to lawyers to either visit that inmate, put money on their books or just to say hello. The individual or individuals that are going home then gives away their items of extra shirts, socks, panties, etc. This is not allowed, but it's done anyway. Sometimes, that individual is bum rushed with others asking for their things of left over commissary. After a short period of time, the lucky one going home hears her name on the loud speaker by the sheriff in the tower and the yells and screams you hear of joy is no holds barred. Everybody is screaming. They pass notes to their friends on the other sides of the doors to inform them as well. They let it out, just being that excited. I wished their happiness of screams and yells were for me. I missed my kids so much; words couldn't explain how I felt. It made it even worse that I couldn't talk to them. We needed some type of collect call service on our home phone or for someone to do a quick collect to a correctional billing department. I knew we didn't have any money for that or even knew how to do that, so talking to them was out of the question.

Trying to adjust in my surroundings, I decided to interact with the other women. I felt that I might as well start talking since I wasn't going home just yet. I walked around the upstairs inside of the "cut" and just looked at them individually trying to figure out what kind of story they had to tell.

There were *Martha Stewart*-type women and *Sister Souljah*-type women, racists white women sharing bunk beds with other women of color. I was placed in a dorm with drug addicts, murderers, real scam artists, and drug dealers. From over hearing the stories amongst themselves, if it wasn't crack cocaine, it was crystal meth. Most of the women that were brought in were strung out off crystal meth. They would sleep for days. A few of them would check to see if the new inmate(s) were still breathing because they slept so long and for so many days. It was as if they were in a stupor for at least two weeks straight. They looked bad and would only get up to use the bathroom and when mandatory, like if a guard came in for any reason like for head count, there had to be plenty of yelling just to wake them up. Often times, they would refuse meals from sleeping so much. I don't know much of anything about that drug, but I know it's not good for you and not good to you.

These women were my age and younger, like in their early and mid-20s and looked older with messed up rotted teeth. The front of their teeth were missing and some black with decay. They didn't look like delicate flowers, they looked like hard thorned stems and when they finally would come down from the meth, they ate a lot. Other women were in there for crack and the look the drug left them was just as bad as the meth.

They were jittery, just couldn't be still and their skin was bad as well with spots all over their bodies, head to toe literally. I don't know if it was from shooting up heroin or crack by itself. I dare not ask, just wondered. To make it so bad, most of them were mothers and some of them had husbands. I often wondered what their children thought about their mom being in jail or their husbands. I know I was in the same situation, but some of these women/mothers/wives were back for three and four times and some even went to prison. It was all new to me and I had so many questions in my head about them and since I always wanted to write about women inmates, I had the perfect opportunity. I started opening my mouth and socializing. When women spoke to me, I didn't just give a side smile as usual along with a mean face, I smiled back and would say hey.

      I was trying to get used to their way of operation with the 5 AM head counts. This would be a challenge to me, as I was not comfortable just falling asleep around strange people in a strange place, especially jail. I wasn't used to standing in line, waiting to pick up a tray of food either. This was one of the most degrading things besides having to use the toilet out in the open and showering with a next to nothing shower curtain. The food they served brought tears to my eyes. I felt like I had my own kitchen, I had my own refrigerator. I could eat whenever I wanted, but being here, made me feel like I was nothing and I guess that was what the jails goal was...designed to make you feel like nothing to make you not come back.

      It was a humiliating experience. Like when they did laundry. This consisted of everyone standing in line waiting to exchange their hideous clothes for more hideous clothes. We were actually wearing recycled clothing down to the underclothes with stained panties and dingy sports bras and socks. All they did were wash them, but didn't do a good job of it. Some women placed maxi-pads in their underwear as a lining so they wouldn't "catch anything." People would blatantly jip you and others would jip you in a slick way by talking to the person in front of you and easing their way up to them still talking, then when the guard comes in with a clipboard, you give her your name and show your wrist band with your picture on it with inmate information to assure that you are you, and you had better make sure that wrist band stayed on your arm at all times because if it wasn't, that was a felony charge called escape and some women would actually take a chance and take that wrist band off.

QUIET STORM

In the meantime, while that person that originally jipped you in line, made their way up to the front of the line. They did this when they gave out toilet paper, soap and served food. It was not that serious to me, as I despised the reasons why we were in line and I absolutely despised their food. The hot food was not hot and when you get a luxury like waffles or pancakes, they were hard as rocks and burnt on the edges. All I ate in the beginning was chips and a cookie. I tried to eat the fruit when it didn't have other particles in it and eating cereal during some breakfast, I refused.

Cereal are one of my favorite foods and to me, that was meant to be eaten in the comfort of your own home out on your patio taking advantage of the beautiful early morning dew with a hint of sunlight or in your bed watching cartoons. Those were my ways of eating cereal. Dinnertime wasn't too pleasant either. Seasoning food was not in the jail cookbook. This is where I would eat my saved lunches like the small bag of potato chips, and oatmeal cookie if I didn't eat the cookie for breakfast. People would be so happy to get the food. They would even auction off food there as well just like they did downstairs in the holding cells. It was all strange and I just couldn't believe that I was really there. Even though I was smack dab in the middle of it and I didn't want to focus so much on "home" because it would only have driven me crazy. Jail is such a terrible place to be and I wouldn't wish it on anyone. As bad as this place was to me, I'm sure prison was much worse, but to overhear conversations about prison, most of the women, repeat offenders said that prison was better and that being in jail was actually doing hard time. They said prison was like being at a college campus where you are able to go to the library, you go to classes, and you get better food. I couldn't stand being in this place and to hear them talk about a prison being better than a jail was just as awful. How could they talk like that? This was no joke. We were locked up, away from our loved ones and they were talking about prison being better like we were on a vacation or something. I felt like crying for them and for myself. I wanted to cry for them because they talked like they were comfortable.

They talked like it wasn't a prison or jail at all. They act like it was some sort of resort. It pissed me off at the same time. They would all laugh and joke and I just wanted to cry my eyes out. I suppose they were making the best of their situation, but I couldn't get with it. I wanted so badly to go home to my kids. I wanted so badly to hug and kiss my kids. Hell, even listening to my kids argue as sisters sometimes do and hear the twins whine like they often did would have been music to my ears. It was better than hearing these women talk. Didn't they feel the same way that I did about their loved ones? Didn't they miss them and want to be home like I did? I couldn't take it. I shied away even more and started writing. I wrote about the things I was hearing and had heard. Some of the conversations were "normal" and understandable for me like about their bills, house notes, car notes, and their jobs. They were concerned that if they did not get out sooner that they were going to lose it all and some of them have. They had absolutely nothing to get out and go to. It was rumored that one of the inmates was back for a second time and she lived in a tent by a trailer park in the woods. That was sad. From listening to some of their stories, I do understand why some inmates are angry and bitter. Other conversations consisted of bisexuality, where there were married women there with children that were as they put it "gay for the stay" and others that were just straight up lesbians. I even heard a few talk about having a "baby mama."

    The way that worked was the women on the outside, some of the inmates were in a relationship with, were really pregnant and bisexual. One very loud conversation made me not want to eaves drop anymore was talk about how the lesbians had relations. They asked each other if they ever had sex in this position or in that position and with multiple partners or with a man included or just other women. It was a horrible conversation and it made my ears bleed. I quickly removed myself from that cut with the mattress and all. I did not want to lie down at night amongst that group in particular. They were too much for me. I had to write a note to the night guard to let her know that I moved my bed to another cut. Their conversation did not mix with my Bible reading at night. I was not comfortable at all.

    Shortly after, I started scoping out which women I could possibly hold a conversation with. I saw one woman that didn't look too much older than me. She was a short woman that looked like she had a lot on her mind. She was standing at the top tier just looking around, looked to be in deep thought. I went up to her and asked what they said she did.

QUIET STORM

She answered me with, "they didn't say I did nothing, I did it." I was like "wow" to myself.

Did I want to finish this conversation? She began to tell me about an African guy she used to mess with that took her to her hot point where they got into an altercation because he ripped her clothing so she retaliated, but she was arrested for fabrication on the African guy's part telling the police that she hit him with a beer bottle in his face. There were no marks on his face, but the police took her to jail anyway for aggravated assault. Her name was Sara and she was a 43-year-old Pittsburgh native, but resided in Georgia. She had come in the same time I did.

She commenced to telling me about a second charge. The police labeled it as "escape" from a divergence center where she was temporarily. She worked full-time, but had to reside at the divergence center until her sentenced finished out, but Sara refused to go back to the center because the authority figures that ran the place, according to Sara, were not professional in their positions. They allowed alcohol amongst the tenants, which was forbidden, and they smoked things other than cigarettes or cigars, and her biggest complaint was that the tenants had to give a percentage of their paychecks to the center and the employees mishandled the monies. So, one day coming from work, Sara never returned back to the center and they reported her as an escapee. When she spoke about the African guy and the employees at the center, she spoke with such anger with a mean look on her face, as if she was taken back into the presence of both the African and the center. Boy did she have a mouth on her.

She had heart too and was not afraid of anyone. You could plainly see that, especially when she told me the story about when she was in the holding cell waiting to come to the pod with several other women. In holding, you could use the phone, but there was only one phone and you were supposed to be courteous, but others were not. This one woman in particular, when Sara needed to contact a family member, refused to get off even after she was asked nicely. So Sara went over towards the woman and with her right hand, snatched the phone from the woman and hit her with her left hand, then commenced to beating her with the phone in the right hand. It was a quick beat down for the woman and by

JAILED BY BLOOD: INMATE 798175

the time a guard came in to see what the commotion was all about, everyone, including Sara and the woman was sitting down on the cold bench. The guard asked if there was a problem and no one said a word. Not even the other women that witnessed the whole thing. When she told me that story, I starting calling her a "feisty midget," which fit her 5 feet tall, small built frame. I liked her nerve. She didn't take mess from nobody. I liked her immediately and began to open up to her about my situation. When I told her about Donovan and me getting into trouble the first time that made me a felon, she didn't judge me. Then when I told her about my being a two-time felon *can you believe that...I'm really what society calls a two-time felon. Makes my heart cry.*

    She commented on how low she thought my brothers and dad were and assured me that God was going to deal with them. Sara gave me the Bible verse of Proverbs 26:27. She could recite the whole Bible and explain what it meant. If you gave her a chapter and verse, she knew right away what it said and could explain to you what it meant. If you started reciting a scripture, she would finish it. She knew the Bible thoroughly. For anything I would tell her regarding my life, she would give me a scripture for and explain it to me and it seemed that the scripture pertained to my life wholeheartedly. She kept telling me that I would be out soon and that I was only going to get probation, no prison time. Her words were great and sound good, but being in the situation at that moment, I surely didn't feel that way and didn't want to hear it until I actually saw it. I felt like that because after that court experience, I allowed myself to be discouraged, but Sara continued to be optimistic on my behalf. She was a cool spirit and I liked talking to her because she was "real" with no phoniness or drama. We realized that thus far, we were the only two that were totally "straight" no bisexual nonsense or "gayfer" mess. She spoke her mind and meant what she said. As the days went by, Sara and I talked more and more and began playing scrabble or playing cards. Spades was the main card game in jail. I didn't know how to play too well until Sara taught me. Before you knew it, we were playing on teams against other inmates and even winning some games.

    It became addictive to me and just for the moments of playing, it actually didn't feel like I was "locked up" because I was enjoying myself. I almost forgot where I was because most of the spade playing game was filled with laughter and tears in our eyes from laughing so hard.

In my mind, I would catch myself and feel bad because I thought about my kids and would say to myself, this was wrong to laugh when they were at home missing me and taking on the house, bills, and each other. I felt guilty for laughing when deep down I was actually crying and dying inside. I don't know if feeling that way was an okay thing or not. I just knew that I wanted so badly to be home with my family and to make things worse; I haven't had a chance to talk to them yet. I almost didn't want to because I knew it would make the situation worse for them and me and them being by themselves without me and me being where I was, it wouldn't be a good thing to talk to them. I felt like it would be a teaser on both sides, but I couldn't be selfish and make that decision for them either.

As I started opening up more, I noticed a young lady that was very quiet. She was across from Sara's top bunk. We would catch glances at one another, but never said anything to each other, so I decided to go to her bunk and talk to her. I don't quite remember what I said, but we just started talking to each other and before I knew it, we went from talking from the top tier to downstairs at one of the tables. She introduced herself as Lorraine. Lorraine was a 22-year-old who was caught shoplifting at a major grocery store.

She arrived about two weeks or so before me. She was a young mother with two children, a little boy and girl, and had just learned that she was four weeks pregnant with her third child. We talked for several hours, listening to each other's problems and giving each other advice. Just like with Sara, I enjoyed talking with Lorraine too. She was a sweet girl and she recognized her problem with an addiction to stealing when she really didn't have to. We started talking about everything from our ex's, families, and the reasons why we were there. Before we knew it, it was time for lockdown.

We had talked for so many hours and didn't realize the time. We went back upstairs to our bunks and I lied down in my usual manner of keeping the slippers on my feet and the whole gear on
my body. Not that I was concerned about anyone stealing them, of which were most cases, but I was not comfortable there and couldn't fathom

the idea of getting comfortable by changing into their nightgowns and going to bed like everything was alright as if I were home. I just couldn't pull myself to do it. If it weren't too cold, which at times, it often would be; I would lie on top of the bed always reading the Bible. I read the Bible a lot. It wasn't something that was new to me. I wasn't one of those inmates they talked about that waited until they got into trouble to pick up the Good Book. I always called on Jesus, but I ain't gonna lie, I called on Jesus even more and even harder since I been there. I lived each moment in disbelief, especially when at lockdown. You would hear women from the bottom tier and top tier having sexual relations with one another.

    It was so disgusting to hear and to even know that it was actually going on made it even worse. My first thoughts were where in the hell were the guards that walked through every hour on the hour and what about the guard in the tower that had camera access to each dorm. I didn't want to hear that mess in the middle of the night. It was terrible. Moans and groans between women. Just sinful. Other inmates didn't speak on it at the time it was going on, not even the ones that were lying next to the inmates that were performing the act and you would think they would be the first to say something, but in this jail and just like others I'm sure, a majority of the females in custody were gay. Sodom and Gomorrah is what I called where I was, right smack dab in the middle of it. I prayed for the covering of the blood of Christ. At night, I would do my hardest praying and the most tear shedding. I cried like a baby. This is when I would put the covers over my face and try to cry as silently as I could in hopes that no one would hear me. At night were the worse times for me because I was sleeping away from my children and we were by ourselves without each other. I couldn't stop thinking about them. I made a mental note that when morning came, I would try our phone number to see if I would be able to get through. I knew it was a long shot because the kids didn't know anything about putting correctional billing on our phone, but just to dial my home number somehow in my own mind would make me feel better.

    Morning came at about 5AM and you hear the same announcement for head count and to be by your bunks. Afterward, it would be a few more hours for what they call breakfast. In between that time is where I got the most sleep with no dreams. I had no dreams being in that place, but I thought about my kids very heavily. After I got my rest, I went to the phones and dialed my number and I got the recording that my phone did not have that service. Then I decided to try my mom's number and I got through.

    I could hear her pick up and say hello, but then a recording butted in to let her know that she had a call from a county inmate. She accepted the call and I cried like a baby to my mom on the phone. At this breaking moment I endured, I didn't care who saw me or heard me. She asked me how did I know to call because she has been trying to get a message to me through the guards to tell me to call, but they refused her. I told her that I just had an instinct to at least try. She then began to run everything down to me of what was going on, but not before she asked me if I was okay. I told her that I was fine for the moment and just like everyone else, wanted to go home. She then ordered me to stop crying and to never cry again while being in this place and I tried to suck it up as best as I could. Mother told me that Craig and Jason have been sending my kids instant messages calling them bitches and whores and even more messed up words of "that's why your mom is in jail" and they have also been putting bad reviews on the review board of Barnes and Noble website commenting on two of my books. They talked about revenge and karma. That was so hurtful to me to know that my own brothers would do what they have done to me and to go even further and send messages like those to my daughters, their own nieces.

    What was worse for me was not the fact that I was in jail, but the fact that my kids were subject to this kind of abuse and had to go through this by themselves and there was nothing I could do for them. It hurt more because I wasn't able to talk to them. I really needed to hear their voices. My mom was telling me everything that she had heard about my case through my lawyer and Mrs. Lisa. It was all very disappointing to everyone. Then she said she received a call from Donovan, my twins' father. He told her that if she had a chance to talk to me to let me know that he loved me. He also said that he would go to my house and stay there with the kids until I got home. At that time, it sure sounded good to me. He also told her to tell me to put his name on my visitor list so he could come see me and that he was going to put money on my books.

JAILED BY BLOOD: INMATE 798175

Donovan and Ryan, my ex-husband and 3 older girls' father, heard about me being in jail via Craig, who thought that he would have me end up with nothing, including my kids by calling their fathers, pretending to be a detective and telling them that I was in jail for identity theft, so they needed to take their children into custody. Little did Craig know, their fathers' and I are on good terms and I already told them that I was having problems with Craig, so when they received the call, they knew right away who it was and hung up on him. After that, Donovan and Ryan called each other, according to mother, and stated that they knew how hard I worked to have a home for our children, so they sent money to the girls to help out with bills and assured me through my mom that they had no intentions on taking my children away from me and Ryan sent message to tell me he loved me.

    I placed Donovan on my visitor's list and a week later, he showed up, twice a week and it made me feel so good to see him. He told me he loved me and stated how much he hated to see me in that position and how much of a coward and a punk he thought Craig was to do something like this. My heart felt overwhelmed. Donovan said that he would continue to call the kids everyday to make sure they were all right. He even put $50 on my books. Then we discussed him going to my house until I got out of jail, and even though it sound like a great idea, it couldn't be done because Donovan was still on probation from our incident several years ago. We doubted very much probation would allow him to leave and live in another state until I got out of jail. We knew that wasn't going to fly, so we just looked at other alternatives of getting back together after all this was over.

    After receiving several visits from Donovan, with a court appearance from my lawyer in between that time period, the visits began becoming not so sincere. It started feeling more like motives again, much like how it used to be back when we were off and on in our relationship. I started to get those same hurt feelings again much like the ones I had before I left Georgia, which was the very reason why I left whereas Donovan wasn't really in my corner.

    He was looking to get something out of my bad situation. His attitude went back to what I known him to be: devious and slick. Anything genuine had gone out the window. It was always a motive with him. He stated to me that he had a girlfriend and he can't just up and leave to go to my house knowing he is still on probation. He acted as if I asked him when he actually volunteered and made note of it to my mother. He then let me know that he was not obligated to come visit me. These ungrateful words coming from someone whom I took time to bail him out of jail behind other females when we were not even together. I was there for him, a phone call away, and this was the thanks that I got. Then he had the nerve to bring up the plea bargain that was made from the prosecutor to my lawyer of doing a year in jail with five years probation. At this time, I was going on 2.5 months and my children were due to start school in August. My oldest was due to go back to college, which left the twins without anyone to watch them. I had to get home ASAP.

Donovan stated that since the prosecutor proposed doing a year, which meant six months because at the time, the county did a 2-for-1 (like 1 month would be equivalent to 2 months time served) and since I was going on my third month, I may as well stay and finish it up, which meant I wouldn't get home until November around Thanksgiving time. I couldn't believe he spoke those words to me (this coming from someone that I would run around like a damn fool collecting money, along with my own money to bail him out of jail on several occasions). He actually told me, the mother of his children, to stay in jail for a year. I kept my cool because I really wanted to come through that triple-paned glass window on him for allowing those words to roll off his tongue so easy. I just looked at him with disgust and said I had to get home to my children because they needed me, then remarked that I knew the real Donovan was going to show up sooner or later, especially when he told me that he felt that I should cancel the child support process on him. I later found out that this was at the suggestion of Craig, who told Donovan to try an get me to cancel since I was at, in their words and thoughts, a "weak point" in my life. He actually talked to Craig and did what he told him, knowing that Craig was the one that put me in jail out of revenge. At this point, I was very disgusted with Donovan and really didn't care if he didn't come to visit anymore. I was already still at the devastating stage of actually being in jail and to have my children's father tell me to stay in jail and cancel child support proceedings was like whoa. I felt so alone.

JAILED BY BLOOD: INMATE 798175

Inmates

Hebrews 13:3

After being delivered that blow-by-blow combination from Donovan, our visit was seized by the silence of the phones being shut down. We both walked away and I did not look back. I went back to the dorm and told Sara and Lorraine what took place and they just looked with disgust and began giving me good advice. We then tried to think on a more positive note to take my mind off what just occurred and decided to play a game of spades. Lorraine was merely new to the game, so Sara taught Lorraine how to play. After our lesson, we realized we needed a fourth person to join in. We noticed an open braided shoulder length, medium-height, slender young lady that actually made it up these stairs around the same time as Sara and myself and asked her if she wanted to play. Sara asked this yellow hair braided, introverted, stoned-faced female her name and she stated with a straight face, which never seemed to smile, "Goldie." She looked like she had a story to tell. Goldie was always so serious and looked to be in deep thought constantly.

After playing a few hands, we began the conversation by asking Goldie why she was locked up. She proceeded, like she didn't have a problem with it, and stated she was trespassing. That was one charge, a misdemeanor, from kicking in the door of an ex-boyfriend. Another charge was failure to pay fines of $8000 from another state after catching a case with an estranged husband on a drug trafficking charge. She was waiting to be expedited. From listening to her talk, she has been to at least two different jails thus far and started telling more about how those jails operated. While she was talking about the jails, she always looked mean. She almost acted as if she had a chip on her shoulder. She was just so angry.

A few hours passed and playing spades became tiresome to me and I wanted to quit. I let my new player partners know that I was going to the phones before taking a nap to try my mother's phone in hopes that we can do a three-way to my phone to talk to my kids. To be able to hear their voices would really make my heart happy. I dialed mother's number, waited and listened to the demeaning recorded message it gives in letting the party your calling know that your an inmate calling collect. Mother accepted and it was nice to hear her voice. After we talked for a few minutes, I asked her to do a three-way with calling the kids on her cell phone, putting them on speaker and putting her house phone up to her cell phone so the kids and I could talk, as best we could, since doing a three-way the regular way, your phone conversation would be cut short with dead silence.

It was awkward, but it worked and I heard my kids' voices. I cried and so did they. Oh how I wished I could come through the phone and just hold them, smell them, and kiss them, but at least hearing their voices held me over for a while because it made me a little stronger and I felt like I could deal with my current situation better. I felt happy and what I felt on the inside, showed on the outside because when I got off the phone with them after talking for about 20 minutes, Sara looked at me with a smile and said, "You talked to your kids didn't you?" I told her yes with a big smile back.

I missed my kids so much that words couldn't explain. I went to the bunk (I hate saying that, "my bunk") and tried to lay down for the night, as I tried to smooth my time in this place by sleeping my days away and staying up to read the Bible at night, but after talking to the kids, I couldn't sleep at all and I was not going back to the "gambling house" the nickname they called playing spades, which was in the dayroom, a few feet away from the bunk beds. I decided to read the Bible and thank God for allowing me to speak with my children. I read the Bible until I fell asleep, which was for over an hour and I fell asleep praying and thanking God just to be awakened by Sara nudging me to let me know it was "chow time." I didn't want their unseasoned, bland, burnt and/or runny meals they served. I just wanted to read, pray, and think about my kids.

I just wanted to think about being home with them doing our routine, lying in my bed watching a movie with a twin lying on each side of me. My eldest daughter would be lying across the bottom of my bed wrapped up in her blanket, and Summer and Nevaeh would be lying on the floor at the foot of my bed wrapped up in their blankets and our snacks of chips (gotta have potato chips), ice cream, sometimes cookies and popcorn, just enjoying our quality time. Most times, we wouldn't even answer the phone. This would be our Sundays after church and sometimes Saturday nights.

Yes, the weekends would be the hardest for me in that place. I despised it. For every weekend that came, I wanted to cry the most, but I would wait til shower time (when the guard would yell "yard call,") I would jump in their not so much of a shower and just let the water run down my face along with my many tears. It was never like the feeling would go away, so I always had tears and hurt feelings to fill me up throughout the days and nights. It was easy to go crazy in there. Just lose your mind. There were plenty of times where I wanted to do just that with screaming. I just couldn't believe nor did I want to digest actually being in jail, or had I already digested the fact with my overwhelming desires to let it all loose? I was being broken and it didn't feel good at all because I could feel every split second of my wants and needs to be home with my children. If I was feeling like this, I could only imagine what they were feeling until I started receiving letters from them.

They were telling me how much they missed me, loved me, and believed that I would be coming home real soon. Their letters were spiritual and uplifting, but then the reality of unbelievable news would hit, like how my mother and oldest brother were planning for my kids to live with them in Illinois. According to my kids, they were told not to pay another house utility, car payment or rent. They told them to keep the paychecks and pack up to go live with them. I don't know what they were thinking to actually present an idea like that to my kids. Maybe they were thinking along the lines of they could help take care of them better if they were closer...I really didn't know or understood, just was trying to make light of it. My kids and I were on the same page with our thought process of NO WAY! They stopped accepting my mother and brother's calls and went as far as having a guard come to me with a note to say "your daughter said to call home, there was an emergency." Now, I knew that the girls didn't have correctional billing on our home phone and I thought they didn't know how to obtain it, but they did. Summer used her babysitting money and placed it on our phone so I could call them directly instead of going through my mother with her cell phone.

QUIET STORM

God had His hands on us. When I got that message from a guard, knowing that they do not relay messages to any inmates no matter what, I knew it was God. I excitedly went to the phones instead of eating their breakfast and dialed my home number...it went through just fine when I heard my daughter pick up and the county gave their "inmate collect calling" speech. When I heard their voices and Summer yelling for the others to come into the room, "mommy is on the phone." She put me on speaker and I heard their voices...all of them and boy, oh boy, my cup runneth over. I felt like I was steps closer to being home. Our time was limited because we didn't want to eat up all the $50 that Summer placed on the call. We wanted to save some time for the rest of the week, so I promised to call every other day. They ran it all down to me again with a caption of how they felt like "nanny" and "Uncle Daniel" were liars and couldn't be trusted. They let me know that they stopped answering their calls. My babies told me to not worry about anything. They assured me that they were all right. Summer and my eldest daughter were working in split shifts performing my work duties of editing reports and staying on top of bills by paying them online and if they didn't have the money just then, they knew how to call and pretend to be me and ask for an extension. They already knew my social security number and date of birth if needed for utilities. They let me know that two young men by the names of Tyrone and Marquez (I considered them to be my sons and loved them and treated them as if they were) from our church were continuing to potty train my son, JJ by bribing him with candy in exchange for going to the bathroom while the girls potty trained LJ. They had their license and would drive my truck and take my kids to church on Sunday and youth night on Fridays and even take them to pay rent at the real estate agents office and go to the grocery store. My girls couldn't drive yet nor did they have a permit, let alone license. Those boys were such a big help and much needed. After we ended the call with a thousand "I love you's" and "miss you's" and "your coming home, declare it in the name of Jesus" according to my kids, I went back to the bunk feeling like a weight was lifted off my shoulders. God has taken over. I felt good inside.

As I was sitting on the bunk bed soaking in my moment of happiness, I grabbed my pen and pad. I was inspired to write more. I took my time and looked around me, trying to imagine why these women were inmates. I mean, I knew my story, as simple as it was, but what was their story? Were they mothers, wives or girlfriends? How did their loved ones take their being locked up. How long were they going to be locked up? I didn't want to guess anymore, so I started to open up a little and approached the ones that my spirit felt okay with and told them that I was a writer and I wanted to make the best out of my stay and I wanted to write about women inmates. To the ones I approached, they were very receptive to it, even the ones that I didn't approach, came to me because what I was doing had spread quickly.

Everyone seemed to like the idea and started throwing stuff at me like, "write about the bad conditions of this jail." "Write about how terrible they treat inmates" and "the staph that is going around throughout the men and women dorms" and the list went on and on and on. I started at the beginning: how they survived. It was definitely a whole other world in there. They would use the insides of the maxi pads that were given as Q-tips to clean out their ears because Q-tips were not allowed. Red kool-offs, a generic of Kool-Aid, would be used on the lips to get the appearance of wearing lipstick and ink pens were used for eyeliner and to draw on eyebrows for when someone had a court appearance so they would look presentable and feel pretty. They would get their hair done the night before with Vaseline to be used as grease and torn pieces of twisted newspaper to take the place of rollers to make their hair curly, that was usually for the white girls, but it did look nice. Now, for the black women, they would have it braided up real nice because there were several women in there that could do some hair with really nice braided hairstyles and others would have updo's and because hair gel was not allowed, jelly from jelly packets and syrup saved from breakfast would take the place of gel, and as crazy as it may sound, the hair was hooked up and looked as if they just came from a salon with it shining and all, not a hair out of place. Me, I would get my hair braided a few days before my court appearances and open the braids the morning of to have that krinkly, kinky look.

Now as far as the food, it wasn't anything to find some women with nearly a loaf of bread saved to be eaten through the middle of the night with butter packs, peanut butter and jelly packs because of hunger pains. As far as keeping busy, they would paint by using the coloring from Skittles (most snacks came from commissary) dipped in water, using empty jelly and butter packets to hold the colored water and tips of pens as the brush. Of course, calendars were made, but I stopped looking at a calendar after my second "can't go home" blow. One of the women there by the name of Esther was an artist and she made a lot of cartoon templates like SpongeBob SquarePants, Tigger, and Winnie the Pooh, just to name a few, before she was released after serving a nine-month sentence for having her second DUI. On her last day, she made little candy baggies for everyone with a nice message, including myself that read, "Dear Storm, I think you are a sweet person and I wish you the best."

There were quite a few women inmates that were "nice" and quite a few that were "not so nice." Thank God, I never had an encounter with anyone, but I have witnessed many altercations over silly things that if we were out on the street, it probably wouldn't mean much of nothing. One inmate in particular, named Lanjile Li Lihanna, they called her "Li Li" for short, was awaiting a trial appeal from a 2005 crime of murdering her then 19-year-old lover after an argument. She has been indicted on charges of malice, murder, felony murder, aggravated battery, and aggravated assault.

The prosecutors were seeking the death penalty, but her public defenders filed an appeal in hopes of a lesser sentence. Li Li was transported for close to three years, spot to spot of all six dorms for more than three and four times, including being placed in isolation, also known as "lockdown," for behavioral problems. She instigating fights, formed a gang with some of the young teenagers and early 20-something inmates, having them do her "dirty work" like beating other inmates up, bullying, stealing from other inmates, etc. She was described as being a cold-hearted individual. She was not admired by other inmates per overhearing frequent conversations about her. She even had death threats from prison inmates that are relatives of the young lady she killed, one of the reasons why Li Li had her lawyers prolong her case as much as possible. Li Li was afraid to go to prison.

She was in the county jail so long; she had privileges from some of the guards that knew her from day one four years ago when she first arrived. What was considered contraband for the rest of the inmates, Li Li was allowed. Things like lip-gloss, regular hair combs from a grocery store, and just simple things that women normally use and need on a daily basis pertaining to hygiene and/or entertainment. When lights out came at around 10 p.m., she and her little followers would be up playing cards, talking loud, laughing loud. Just totally ignorant to the rules and depending on what guard was on duty, nothing would be done about it. The guards would come in for their every hour routine dorm check and they completely bypassed Li Li and her gang members.

They would even ignore complaints of them having lesbian relations. I think they ignored it mostly because a majority of the female guards were gay themselves...just sinful. I witnessed an encounter of her engaging in nasty sexual relations with a 19-year-old, allowing her to eat her out. I was up reading my Bible and heard moans and groans. Her bed was a bottom bunk, catty cornered in the cut across from my top bunk on the other side of the building, but she was visual. I couldn't believe it. I put my back toward them and put my head under the covers, using what little light there was overhead to complete my reading with an interruption of praying, asking God to "please get me outta here!" It was bad enough being there and not knowing when I was going to go home to my kids, but to be there amongst murderers, psychos, and everything else was cruel punishment. This girl had no soul to me. There was a time where I asked an inmate about what she thought my outcome was going to be and she suggested I ask Li Li simply because she has been there longer than anyone in the dorm. I then approached Li Li and told her a little bit about my situation and I noticed that she couldn't look me in the eyes for five seconds. She was looking all around me, talking, explaining to me what she felt was going to happen, of which she was later correct. (My mother said that she couldn't look me in the eyes because of the God in me.) You know how when you're speaking with someone and you can began to get a feel of them, their spirit? Well, I couldn't get anything from her. I could sense nothing; it was almost like she was hollow, empty. I never experienced that from a human being before.

Like most of the inmates, Li Li was taking medication for depression and apparently hallucinations. There was "pill call" every single day, twice a day (half the women in the dorm were in line for pill call). I remember hearing stories about her from when she was in lockdown, talking to demons. She had a bunkmate and in Li Li's eyes, the demon wanted to disrupt her top bunkmate and Li Li talked to the demon, telling it "no, no, come on back down here, leave her alone." Wow, is all I can say to that. Later, the county superior court judge sentenced Lanjile Li Lihanna to life in prison without the possibility of parole. The D.A. suggested that she should not be allowed out of solitary confinement when she enters the state prison system.

Among other inmates, there were some that were even big time drug smugglers, like one young lady that went by the nickname of "Chi-Chi." This was her third trafficking charge. Her first charge carries a minimum of 20 years depending on the grams of which she had at that time, 64 pounds of cocaine. Chi-Chi never did any time on her first and second charges. The other inmates labeled her as a snitch in order for her to stay out of jail because she would get late night visits from her lawyer at close to 11PM and at times, would not come back until 1 a.m. Now everyone knew that attorney visits were only allowed during visiting hours, but Chi-Chi's attorney would send for her even during the weekend in the late night hours. They would meet up in the jail library.

She would come back chewing gum, which was not allowed and considered contraband, she would even smell like cigarettes, and she would come back with either wearing a gold band and sometimes not wearing a gold wedding band. No one knew what that was about, but with all the secret meetings and doing who knows what in that library with her female "attorney" she was denied a bond, which was $250,000. Her goal of becoming free was looking a little cloudy. Looks like Chi-Chi was finally going to get some real prison time.

One woman, named Willa, 36, was facing 35 years in prison for shoplifting. She stated that she was not really the one shoplifting. She was only driving and had no idea that the person she was with was stealing. Willa had a husband and several small children. The youngest was 7-months old. Often you would hear her on the phone cussing her husband out, telling him to "get me the hell out of here." In between her tears, listening to the snide remarks and the inmates laughing at her, I couldn't imagine being in her shoes. Thirty-five years in prison was no joke. There were rumors that her husband, who was a Mexican, took their children to Mexico where he had planned on residing. Rumors were circulating around that if Willa's husband posted her bond of $127,000 that she would run to Mexico. I can't really say I blame her. That's a lot of years of your life gone and too many away from your family. It seemed like shoplifting, or "boosting" is what they called it, was popular next to doing or selling drugs and prostitution. In talking with some of the women, they made a career out of it.

One lady told me she made a living off "boosting." That was her job 24/7. It was how she paid her rent and bills overall. Her name was Rhoda. Rhoda was in jail off a 12-year-old warrant. She got caught from having a busted tail light, went through the old routine pull over and the cop ran her name and found out about the warrant, next thing you know, she was hauled into jail. Back then, the judge that placed that warrant on her had passed away, so she thought for sure that she would get off, but she has been in jail then going on six months. When she finally went to court, they offered her a year in prison with five years probation. She didn't want that deal, as a lot of the inmates didn't want what they would call to be "on papers" referring to the probation. She, as all the others, would rather go to prison to get it over with because in prison, you could get 3 for 1. However, that wasn't Rhoda's case. They wouldn't bend and she was sent to prison, but not given 3 for 1. A law was passed and they stopped prison 3 for 1 and county jails 2 for 1. This time when you were sentenced to however many years, you did exactly those many years, no exceptions.

As time went by and most of the inmates knew that I was an editor, they wanted me to use my grammar and penmanship to write letters to their lawyers to question their cases. Some days, I was writing up to two to three letters per day. I didn't mind at all, as it helped pass time. While I was at it, I decided to write a few letters to my lawyer to see what was up with my case. I didn't hear from him on a daily basis like I, and everyone else, thought I should.

Every time I wrote, I never received a response and I would only get a visit if he heard something about my case, which seemed to be not too often. It was already going on 2.5 months and I think I saw him maybe three times in the very beginning. I didn't know what to think, but I knew I was beyond homesick.

My surroundings were more than overwhelming to handle. Although any inmate I came into contact with was cool with me, I was still surrounded by strangers. It was not home, they were not my family. I was tired of the younger teenaged inmates disrespect to everyone with the nonstop noise that came along with their every third word being a cuss word, the stealing of other inmates, especially new inmates commissary and the overall inmates behavior of both young and old of fist fighting, cussing each other out. Older white inmates showed their very open racism, two-faced, back stabbing, and the kissing the guards' butts. To top things off, most of the women would refer to each as "bitch" and they said it as if they were calling each other's real name, like "bitch, guess what?" or "bitch, how you doing?" I couldn't stand it. There was so much to deal with and not to mention the shakedowns that could go on at any hour of the night. It could be 2 o'clock in the morning and the guards would come in and yell with their man voices and demand you to get up out your bunk and strip your bed of the sheets and blankets and take the ultra thin mattress off the bunk and throw it on the floor so they can go through your sheets with the end of their billy clubs.

Now as if that wasn't enough, you had to clear out what they called your "cubby" that had your personal items like deodorant, toilet paper, pads, soap and sometimes food from commissary and they went through that with their billy clubs too. Occasionally, you would hear a few new inmates ask what the problem was, but the ones that have been there for a while, would inform them because the guards certainly would not. After the little escapade, they would walk out and tell you to clean up the mess and get back to bed, but you had to do it in the dark because they turned the lights back out. The only beam you would get was from the dim light in the toilet area and you were out of luck if your bunk was not close to the toilet.

Being in that place was hard to cope with. I was told a story that just before I got there, a woman tried to kill herself more than once by jumping down from the top tier. She would throw herself over the balcony. The first time she tried to kill herself, she went to a fellow inmate and told her that she was feeling "down" and that inmate tried to find a scripture to help uplift her. A scripture that she knew like the back of her hand, but wanted to have a visual for the young lady so she could read it for herself and the devil was busy at that moment because that fellow inmate could not find that scripture for nothing in the world until after she heard a loud thump that was actually heard in the dorm next door. The young lady jumped and bounced from landing on her back. Now you would think that the infirmary would keep her there or take her to a local hospital, but they didn't.

    They placed her back in the dorm and she made another attempt of suicide. This time, she broke her back. This time, she was kept in the infirmary, but not taken care of by the nurses, as maggots ate a hole in her head and her bandages were not changed. I'm not sure how long she was an inmate, but it was obviously too long for her. She was only in jail for unpaid traffic tickets. She was in one of those halo braces and a wheelchair. After her time was up and she had her court date, all charges were dropped against her. There were rumors that her parents were suing the county jail.

    A lot of the women were there for prostitution, drug selling, drug using, shoplifting, and just because of tickets. One lady was there so long for a traffic ticket that her estranged husband tried to obtain full custody of their five-year-old son, but with the help of her
Lawyer, she fought and negotiated so well that she was released and her estranged husband never gained custody. There were talks about how the county jail would keep you longer than they were supposed to for financial gain. That jail, in particular, was a privately owned jail and received just about $100 per day per inmate. There was one incident where the police had actually picked up an elderly woman that looked to be in her late 50s or early 60s. She was intoxicated, sure enough, but she was two doors away from her house and was walking. Instead of acting like a human being with a heart, they actually hauled her in. She was pitiful to look at and you couldn't help but to feel sorry for her. She would put you in the mind of your grandmother. She was very upset.

    Some of the women approached this sweet-looking older woman and began to just converse with her to take her mind off of things and tried to make her laugh while the other would redo her hair to make her look presentable for first appearance, which she was let go without bond.

One woman came in during the middle of the night from what she states, "her dog was barking too loud." She had complaints from neighbors, so the officers asked her for the paperwork she would have when she first purchased her dog and she couldn't find it quick enough, so they placed her under arrest and called it disturbing the peace. She was bonded out the next day after her family member found the paperwork for the canine. It was rumored that the county jail would throw people in jail for small things that didn't make any sense in order for the police to make a quota and for the county to make their money from how many inmates they housed.

Then there was the question of how clean the jail was, which it was not. There were brown recluse spiders lurking around the dorms, as well as unidentified bugs and a breakout of staph that several inmates had. I was told about a news crew that came from tips about how dirty the place was and still is. There was more talk of how the Feds were supposed to take over, but I think it was more of a myth. Even though all the negativity was overwhelming, there were a few good things that went on in there. On a daily basis, they had an old pop tart box with prayers inside that actually were torn out of a daily prayer book. Someone would go around and offer you a "blessing" and you take one of those folded blessings and read your scripture with a cross reference of the Bible. It was a nice change. Whenever it was anyone's birthday, they would make cakes out of the peanut butter from peanut butter cookies, scraping off the cream, mixing it in with milk and stirring it up with the end of a pencil. They would use whatever else ingredient they utilized with a chocolate covering for the icing. They were very creative. On occasion, the dorms would hold talent shows and they made you forget where you were for a second. It was fun and enjoyable to watch. There was a lot of talent behind those bars, and on a daily basis, every night between 8 o'clock in the evening, a woman in her mid-30s, by the name of Arlene, would hold church/prayer service in the dorm for all who wanted to join. I was surprised at all who joined in and held hands in that circle of prayer.

JAILED BY BLOOD: INMATE 798175

They were tearing up, some crying out all their emotions. Arlene would start service off with belting out in her beautiful gospel singing voice a church song and most of all the inmates in that dorm would gather and hold hands in the circle and listen to the reading of scriptures, preaching, and prayer. At the end of service, we would say what we would like prayer about and they would stay positive, for instance, if someone had a court date coming up, they would say, "such and such is going home on that court date." We all would give each other a hug while wiping away tears, and then at lights out, you would hear throughout the dorm, "I love yous" and "good nights" from each other. Underneath all the rough surface of many, I looked a little deeper and saw women, mothers, sisters, and friends.

Isolation

Psalm 102:7

I received my latest blow in court. I did not get the opportunity to see the judge again. I was made to sit down in intake for hours after getting up at 3 a.m. They prepared that next to nothing breakfast, was forced to listen to ungodly conversations, put on that dreaded bus, and taken back down to the courthouse freezing cold basement where I was, along with others, disappointed in knowing that the county jail was again our current residence for a little while longer. After getting back to the dorm, I was too choked up for words. I didn't talk much at all to Sara, Lorraine or Goldie. I spoke briefly about what happened, got on the phone talked to my kids and my mom, though they already knew what the outcome was because of my lawyer. Afterward, I went to my bunk and tried to get as comfortable as I could because I had sores and bruises on my legs and my thighs from the thinness of the mattress pad that felt more like I was actually lying on the metal bunk itself, so I lied down on my back with the covers over my head and cried like a baby in silence.

I refused dinner and waited for lights out to analyze what took place that morning. I thought about my kids. I thought about my business. I thought about our home. I thought about my present status. What was I going to do? I was at my lowest point ever in my life. I felt helpless and so not in control of my life. Now I have always been a woman of prayer, so I did what I knew best and that was to read the Bible and have a talk with God. I began to read the Bible given to me from the "church lady" that came on Mondays. I started from the very beginning with plans of reading it to the very end.

I began reading after 5AM head count and continued reading during breakfast chow time. I did not eat; I would get in line for the tray and give it away or trade it for their snack bags of chips or a cookie. I did this at every chow time of breakfast, lunch, and dinner. I stayed on that top bunk and kept my head buried in that "Good Book" and refused playing spades, scrabble or even indulging in conversation. I never went outside, which was a teaser anyway and I never signed up to go to the law library. Now as I mentioned before, I was no stranger to the Bible. When I was home, I read it on a daily basis, but for some reason, being in that place, I more so understood every word written and saw how it applied to my life ever since the day I was born and even before then. I felt a since of calmness. I did not worry anymore about when I was going home. I just felt a desire to continue to read and get more in depth with what God was telling me through His words.

As I was reading, I felt like He was actually talking to me and me only. I began to let go of the horrible words that kept playing back in my mind like when my dad stated that he didn't care what happened to me after he told my lawyer that he gave me permission to use his name and social, but now, he wanted money. He thought that when I was fined for the gas bill and his cellphone bills that he was going to get the money in his hand, but little did he know that the money was going to the collection agencies to pay off the bills. My lawyer told me, "I hate to say it, but your dad is an asshole." I even heard that he emailed my mother and told her to put the money in a bag and place it in a Wal-Mart shopping cart so Craig can pick it up. He stated that he wanted exactly $3000.00. His own brothers and sisters (my uncles and aunts) told him how horrible of a person and how wrong he was to do this to me, his own daughter, but his response was that he just did not care, like father like son. It was like when I called Jason to ask him if he could talk to Craig to get him to call the whole thing off by calling back the Atlanta Police since he called them and pretended to be our dad to press charges, couldn't he call and pretend to be our dad again and say never mind. Jason's words to me were, "he ain't gonna do it, so you might as well get used to eating pussy," then he laughed and hung up on me, then Craig called me a few minutes afterward and I pleaded with him to call the whole thing off and his words to me were, "you should have just put her and her kids out (referring to his wife and her children) and not me and my son, so just deal with it." That was a lot to swallow, but I learned to swallow it and really forgive my brothers and father with a genuine attitude. I have forgiven them, to this day, without any hateful feelings towards either one of them. I learned that I could forgive them and still love them from afar.

QUIET STORM

In the meantime, I began to read before breakfast and filled up on studying. I made a routine to read after head count; sleep the rest of the day and stay up reading all night. I would begin to compare Bibles and a fellow inmate would receive Joyce Meyer books in the mail. She was kind enough to share them with me and I began reading her books front to back and cross-referenced to the Bible. I started taking notes that played a part in my current situation and I began to understand the scriptures more and more. I really enjoyed it. I was amazed by it and excited about it. I always prayed no matter what and talked to God when I took a drive anywhere or making dinner. It was just a daily routine in my life back home, so I learned that it was okay to adopt that routine at my present residence. I would write letters to God and began thanking Him five and six times a day or more. I would make the rest of my time there go as quick as I could by writing letters to God, reading and studying the Bible, taking notes, and writing this book. Before I realized it, I was on a spiritual fast and I isolated myself and began to live in my own world far away from where I actually was and for the first time of being in jail, I felt at peace.

Court

Deuteronomy 17:9

July 31, 2007 at 1:30 pm, I had another court appearance that I prayed would be my last. I went through the same long routine of a 3AM wake up call, though I was already awake. I was taken down to intake and spent four hours in the small cell with one cold metal bench and at least 20 women, listening to cries, prayers, church songs, and gossip until breakfast. An hour later, the buses and patty wagons came to take us to court in downtown Sparta where I sat for a few more hours after being body searched and placed in another cold, small cell where I had to wait a few more hours until it was time for my case to come up. For some reason, on this particular day, I felt good. I mean real good. I had no worries. The day before, Sara kept telling me, "Storm, I been praying for you and girl, your going home my sistah." I believed her. I felt it just as much as she did.

All that week, people were asking me if I was going home and all I could say was, "Lord willing." I had hope. I felt it in my gut. I was finally going home to my babies. I honestly believe that the process took as long as it did not because for felonies you have to stay for three months, but because God was trying to tell me something. He wanted me to experience this so I could have a story to tell, as well as others. He wanted me to learn how to genuinely forgive and love your enemies and not just say that you do. He also answered my prayers in allowing me inside to write about other women like I always wanted to do. He also showed me never to judge anyone about anything, but to help them if I can. From the time I came here, the women would ask me about myself and asked why I was here and I told them my story and what my life was like at home with my kids, business and my book writing.

They would say, "It was meant for you to be here. God has a plan for you." I remember thinking, "what are they talking about, it was meant for me to be here?" It would make me kind of mad for them to say it because I didn't want to be here, but now I understand. I understood it all. The guard came down to the basement-holding cell and read my name out loud along with a few other inmates, as it was time for us to make our appearances in front of the judge. We were escorted with our bling chains to a small room, waiting for our case to be called. My lawyer walks in from a side door of the courtroom and brings me paperwork and told me to sign here and there and initial this and that. He said, "You ready to go home?"...in my mind I was like, "hell yeah," but I said, "yes, I am" with a sweet smile on my face. After I signed the paperwork, he told me to get ready to see the judge.

It was same judge that sentenced me the first time back in 2003 when Donovan and I got into trouble for writing a bad check. My lawyer went back into the courtroom and I had a chance to sneak a peek at my kids' pictures that I kept in my shirt pocket. A sheriff came into the small room where I was and walked me into the courtroom and there he was, Judge Bonnard, well known as one of the meanest and strictest judges in Sparta. He aged since 2003 with his entire hair gray this time. He looked a little plumper too. He began to talk and gave his same "scare tactic" speech about how he doesn't like people from jail and talked about his old war stories, and blah, blah, blah.

Back then, he scared the mess out of me, but this time, I could care less about what he was talking about. I just wanted to get home. He was not fazing me at all. I held my head high in that courtroom with confidence, shackled with the prosecutor on one side and my lawyer on the other, as I listened to the prosecutor butcher my character by telling the judge why I was there. When he was reading about my case, it sounded so horrible. He made me sound like a career criminal, especially with my prior, but he was doing his job I guess. Couldn't really be mad at him, but my thought process listening to this man was like "I really wish he would shut the hell up." One thing I can't stand is to be judged. There were others in the audience, and black people at that, I never saw before and we don't know each other true enough, but I can imagine what they were thinking just listening to this man talk about me.

I was starting to feel embarrassed and the white people that were in the audience, I knew they were already thinking negative about me from their glares alone...so messed up. I was just so ready to go. Out of all the negativity that was being heed to, the judge heard one good thing...I turned myself in. He commended me on that so my lawyer thought it would be a good time to come in with an interruption of placing a little brag on me about the books I wrote and the book I was working on for cancer survivors. I began to feel a moment of relief until the prosecutor started doing his job again. He and my lawyer got into a small under the breath disagreement about rather or not to let the judge know of my positive accomplishments. The prosecutor cut my lawyer off and said, "Let's just let it go because he seems to be pleased with her right now and we don't want to make him angry."

My lawyer and I glanced at each other because we both knew what was going on, so he just left it at that and in two seconds, my case was done, but not just before the judge asked me, "why not fight it?" (inmates have asked me the same thing) now that was certainly something to think about and it made me ponder for a split second and only a split second, but I lost too much already and I quickly told him, "I had to get home to my children." Even though I played off that question, didn't mean I didn't think about it. I mean, if I had the time to do so, I believe I could have won my case because the case they built up against me was mostly of a bluff and threats of having my father come from Israel to testify against me, knowing that they were not going to pay for something like that. Then they changed it from him actually coming back to the states to, "well, we will have him televised" which would have been more money than paying for an actual plane ticket. My case was not high profile where they would even shell out money to do such. Then they said that they were going to have my brother come testify, which the question played in my head of, "What would he actually be testifying to?" He was the one who called the gas company, pretending to be our dad. He would have perjured himself, so that would have been out of the question as well. All in all, the prosecutors really had me in jail for three long months away from my life/children off of a bluff and threatening lies. Now I know that I was in jail for three months, which would probably feel like nothing next to folks in prison, but for me, it was still a messed up ordeal and my kids and I had to adjust to a lot of indifference. After the judge handed me down five years of probation (he canceled my first two years from 2003 and ran it concurrent and added on three more years...I would have been done September of 2008, now I have til August

2012) with a $3000 fine, (I had just paid off my previous fine of $3000 from 2003 in August 2007). I was legally free from the court system, but not physically until many hours later.

I walked over to my Georgia probation officer, who was the wife of my probation officer back in 2003. She said that he recognized my name and told her the positives about me and that was why she wanted me under her supervision. After I signed the paperwork with my probation terms and costs of fines and fees, I was put back out into the small, hot hallway, sweating bullets, still chained up of course, listening to butthead male inmates that were locked away in what looked like a closet, make cat calls for me to come around their way so they could see me. I did not speak a word to them. I just wanted them to shut up and they did when the guard came in and told them to "shut the fuck up." I was able to stand in peace staring at my kids beautiful pictures excited about getting home. I daydreamed about already being at home with them. This time when I did it, I knew that it was actually going to happen...I couldn't wait. After the judge handled cases of two women that were in the patty wagon with me, they signed their paperwork and placed them in the cubby hole too and we managed to hug each other as best we could with the chains on our waist connected to our wrists and wished each other luck. We sat and waited several more hours down underneath the building in a cold cell, waiting for others to have their cases dealt with. Some came back to the cell with disappointing faces, some crying, and others were smiling like us. All you heard was, "you going home? You going home?" I was cheesing my butt off. One young girl was like, "shit I know you going home with that big ol' smile on your face." I didn't even have to say nothing, and didn't.

After everyone was accounted for, they had us line up in single file, just before they body searched us, and loaded up on a tricked out old school bus this time. You could see outside, but they had a wide metal bar across half of the windows with teeny tiny holes in it and the back half of the bus had a caged door to it where male inmates were kept, but you could hardly see them and they could hardly see you. It didn't stop them from talking to you though, but it wasn't allowed, so the guard driving the bus would blast the radio to make it hard of hearing each other and it worked. Everyone started singing to the music and tried dancing around in their couch seat as best they could with being chained up and all. Back out in the county, we sat down in intake in the holding cell for at least another two more hours until shift change, going on 6PM. It was almost chow time. At shift change, a guard escorted us back to the R-pod, unchained us, and everyone dispersed back to whichever dorm they came from. When I got back to my dorm, there was Sara waiting for me at the door with a smile on her face. She said, "you're going home ain't cha sistah?!" I told her, "Yes, thank you Jesus!" She said, "I already knew it that's why I packed up your stuff." Sara had packed up my bed and cleared out my cubby. I gave her all my stuff from toilet paper, hair grease to what food I had left from commissary. Now, all I had to do was wait for the guard in the tower to say, "Storm, pack your bags." I couldn't wait…literally. So I pushed the buzzer to ring the guard in the tower and asked her if she had my name ready yet and she said she had not. She was nice about it.

      I must have buzzed her like three and four times until finally I asked her if I could just wait in the hallway while sitting on the mattress and she laughed and said, "no, I'm sorry, you can't do that." I laughed myself, but I was so serious. To pass time away, I asked Sara and a few other inmates that I became friends with if they wanted to hear my poetry/spoken word and they were more than excited to hear. We sat on Sara's bunk and I belted out with such passion, my poetry. I had two of them literally in tears. They absolutely loved it. The one we called, "Baby Mama" said, "Auntie Pretty, (*that's what she called me*) why didn't you do that in the beginning, everybody would have gotten along better in here." I laughed and told her I was too shy and that I didn't think anyone wanted to hear it. As soon as I recited one poem, they wanted me to do another and another. I was running out of poems, at least the ones I had memorized. Going on my fourth poem, they called my name. It was time for me to get back home. They gave me hugs and promised that when they got out, we would meet up in Miami at a poetry venue so they could watch me on stage. I felt so good and so relieved. I felt like after I recited, I let go of a lot of built up stress. I'm glad I was able to do it. Besides always wanting to write about women inmates, I also always wanted to travel to different women's prisons and recite so they could have something to look forward to and maybe inspire them to write poetry themselves. I had a lot of female poet friends I wanted to travel with me to the women's prison and male poet friends to travel to the men's prisons to recite. Maybe one day, that dream can come true...who knows. It's not a bad idea and it's not entirely impossible.

Anyway, I lugged all the crap they assigned to me like the super thin mattress that was so thin, it gave me battle wounds of bruises all over my thighs and legs from the metal bunk along with their dingy sheets, washcloths, towels, and underclothes. After I dumped all of it inside of what looked like a dumpster, I sat out in the hallway until a guard came to escort me down to intake where I had to change for the last time out of their fine blues and grey into my street clothes that I came in there with. When I was changing, I heard another girl complain about not being able to fit back into her street clothes, so a guard had to get her some type of outfit that looked like a plastic jumpsuit for situations such as that, then they busted her with trying to steal their sports bras and sweat socks. She was crazy. I wasn't about to take any of that dirty laundry home. I wanted to keep jail at jail. She responded to them with "I wanted to take some of the sports bras home to my daughter." I couldn't believe it, but I kept my mouth shut and kept it moving while they finally escorted us out to the front of the building in the waiting area. Now, I don't know how and didn't even know that it was possible, but my cell phone was in with my belongings and I remembered turning it off when I turned myself in, but when I got it back, I turned it on and after three months, it still worked. I mean it still had juice! I thought it was God. I called my kids ASAP, then my mom, and then Mrs. Lisa, who had already known, all of them did, that I was coming home.

JAILED BY BLOOD: INMATE 798175

Going Home

Romans 8:28

Mrs. Lisa had her oldest son to pick me up because she had to work. We were all like family, even to this day. He was right on time, sitting outside waiting on me. I got in the car embarrassed and feeling ashamed. I slumped down in my seat looking out the window with tears rolling down my face, silently appreciating the outdoors. He looked at me and said, "it's all right Storm, I know how you feel, I've been there. It was silence on the way to his mother's house with his occasional glancing over at me to see if I was going to talk. He let me in the house where his younger brother and dad were and led me to the bathroom. I could remember the look on his face of feeling sorry for me. It only made me more embarrassed and the more I wanted to cry. After he left, I took a much-needed shower and put on some fresh clean clothes of mine from my suitcase that I already had at her house from three months ago when I turned myself in. Mrs. Lisa would always cook for her family before going to work and I was so glad she did. She made corn on the cob, ribs, greens and potato salad. I threw down like I never ate food before. Then I got mad at myself because I got full too fast. I lied on her couch and thoughts of still being in jail kept surfacing through my mind. When I would doze off, I had little dreams about still being in there and I would jump up out of my sleep and look around me. To keep my mind clear, I watched a little television, but fell right off to sleep. I had to get some rest too because I had to report to the probation office first thing in the morning, 9AM sharp. Even though I slept on a couch, it was the best rest my body had in three months. Anything was better than that skinny, metal bunk bed.

  The next day came so fast. I called a cab to drop me off at the probation office downtown. When I went in, it brought back memories, not good ones either. Being there brought back a thought process from 2003 when I was on probation for my first offense. The atmosphere sucked then and it still did. I went upstairs and asked for my probation officer and was made to wait because my probation officer was in court. In being there, I had no idea it was going to take as long as it had. I thought I was going to be able to pick up my paperwork of a week pass to go back to Florida and hit the airport because that was what I was told by the probation officer herself in court that day. Not the case. After my wait, her assistant took me to the back and I had to give her my current residence, information, etc. then made to go back to the front and wait again. I got there at 9AM sharp and at this time, it was going on 12:30PM, my mother and kids had already bought me an electronic flight ticket to board at 1PM. The closer it got to my time, the more impatient I became and I was about to blow up. I kept asking the assistant where my probation officer was and that I had a flight to catch.

    At this time, my conversation with her was interrupted by this Uncle Tom nigga who made it well known to me and everyone else in the waiting room that he was the chief there. He pretty much scolded everyone in the room by making this lady throw her water bottle in the trash because he didn't want any beverages in the office at all, even though her water bottle had the top on it. Then he interrupted a woman's private conversation with another person about her trying to get a traveling permit to another state and he told her to change her conversation. Then he continued being a butthead with this guy by asking him who was he there to see, the guy told him, then he asked him what was his reason for being there and when the guy tried to tell him, it wasn't good enough for him. He kept interrupting the man saying, "That is not right, now why are you here?" Dude was a straight up butthead for no reason. When he got to me, he told the assistant to send me to his office. She then followed him back there and I could hear her telling him how impatient I was and how disrespectful she thought I was and added her opinion of how she didn't think I deserved to catch my flight. What a bitch! She had no idea what I had to deal with and been through. My kids were my motivation and the reason for my impatience. I wanted to get home to them so badly. Who in the hell did she think she was to say I didn't deserve to catch my flight.

    He then totally agreed with her and called two other probation officers in his office along with me and tried to make a fool out of me. He kept calling me a criminal and said there was nothing I was going to do about it. He was taunting me and pissing me off at the same time. I told him that I didn't appreciate his name-calling and he pretty much dared me to do something about it by asking me what was I going to do about it. Then he had the nerve to say that he sees "my kind" everyday and couldn't care less about me. (He was such a messed up individual. Talk about giving blacks high positions). I was furious and he knew it and messed with me even more and told me that he was canceling my traveling permit to Florida and that he didn't care that my kids already paid for my ticket. Then said that if I didn't show back up tomorrow morning at 8AM, even though the office did not open until 9AM, that he was going to put me back in jail and told me to leave his office, as well as his building, and when I was walking out, he stopped me and asked what was I in jail for and he continued with, "what selling drugs, doing drugs, theft?" then his voice got deeper and louder and said, "WHAT?!". Can you believe that? He talked down to me and humiliated me on purpose in front of the other probation officers, of whom he made leave their office with clients in it. He ripped up my pass and tossed it toward me in my face and dared me to do something about him calling me a criminal and after all that, he didn't even know why I was there. I just kept my mouth shut after he cut me off and told me that he didn't care about my kids buying my ticket, I was too through then because my blood was over boiled. I wanted to strangle that nigga, but I had to get home to my kids. I looked him in the face with all the probation officers and that bitch of an assistant standing around me and said, "I got a gas bill in my dad's name." He, along with the other officers put their heads down and you could hear a pin drop.

    I fought back every tear that was swelling up in my neck and all he could say, not looking me in the eye, but looking all around me with a quiet tone, no bass in his voice at all anymore was, "just be back here tomorrow morning." I walked out in silence. I got to the front where the receptionist was and she had a look of sympathy on her face for me and whispered, "I'm sorry." I thanked her and walked out. As soon as that door shut behind me and I was outside, I cried like a baby pacing up and down the sidewalk. I was pissed, hurt, humiliated at the same time because there was nothing I could do about it but take it. I called my mom and had her put me on three-way with the girls and I let them know what happened. I was not able to come home just yet. We all were disappointed. I didn't want to talk to them anymore because it hurt too much, so I hung up with them and called Mrs. Lisa to pick me up and told her what happened and she said, "honey, all of them are like that, just let it go," but I couldn't let it go. I just couldn't. I didn't care who he was, he was wrong to treat me like that and prejudge me and not even know my case. He was totally wrong and I refused to let it go. I felt in my heart that I needed to call him and transfer those feelings and that was exactly what I did. I rode with Mrs. Lisa to pick up her mother-in-law to take her shopping and while they were in the grocery stores, I sat on a bench outside the plaza and called that probation office and asked for that man.

    The receptionist transferred the phone call and he answered and I let him know who I was and commenced to telling him that I didn't like how he talked to me and judged me without even knowing my name or why I was even there. He tried to talk and I cut him off this time and asked him to look up my company website and he did surprisingly and he said, "you have your own business?" and I said, "yes since 1997 and I am an author." I told him to look up the major bookstores in the U.S. and put my name in the search bar and my books would show and he did. He was like, "wow, I'm impressed." I then told him to click on a link that had pictures of my kids on it and told him, "That is who I am. My children, my company, and my books were who I am, not a criminal." I then briefed him on my brother setting me up and how I turned myself in and he apologized to me in regards to my brother and father and apologized to me again in regards to what happened less than an hour ago, then he continued on with, "I'm really a nice guy, really sweet, I am." I told him I believed him. He said, "It's just that when we get people that come into the office from the jail, a lot of them have attitude and we treat them all the same, but I'm really a sweet guy." I told him again that I believed him and said, "Everyone that is in jail are not criminals, there really are innocent people locked up and, unfortunately, their innocence is proven much later in life." I then thanked him for apologizing and listening to me and conversing with me. He then thanked me for calling and said he would see me tomorrow at 9AM. instead.

    Whoosh! After that phone call, I felt brand new for a moment. I had to get that off my chest and I'm glad I did. I was proud of myself. I felt a little better to talk to my mom and kids too. I was in a much better mind set. We were still kind of mad about the ticket, but we looked on the brighter side and thought, at least I was not in jail and I was with family, which is exactly how we feel about Mrs. Lisa.

Tomorrow came and at 9AM, Mrs. Lisa dropped me off at the probation office. I walked in there and went straight up those stairs with confidence in hopes that this would be the last time I had to see that place and those people. I went inside, signed my name next to my probation officer's name and waited for her to call me to the back. While I was waiting, the chief came out and made sure I saw him by giving me this big Kool-Aid smile and waving in my face, "hello, how are you?" I was stunned. I laughed to myself and spoke back with a sweet good morning, and then my name was called. I went to the back where they had to take my picture and fingerprint me. This, I was told, was something that they did for all probationers that lived out of state. After all was said and done and I watched the pen smoothly write out on that form, giving me a pass to go back home, the probation officer let me know that I could only go home for a week. My heart dropped. "I was away from my kids for three long months," I explained, "why only a week and not forever?"

She then explained to me that it was their policy. I told her I never heard of that and she proceeded to tell me that after my week pass, I had to return or I would be locked up for violation and as if that wasn't enough, I had to stay in the state of Georgia until my case was transferred and accepted by the state of Florida, which normally took about 45 days to three months, or longer. It didn't matter that I was already on probation in Florida from the first offense back in 2003. She said that because this was a new case, Florida had to accept me all over again. I told her that my home and career, as well as my children were already established in Florida, but this did not matter. Basically, I had a week to get my family moved back to Georgia. At that moment, my world fell apart. I thought it was the end. I cannot explain how pissed I was. How in the hell was I going to tell my kids that we had to move back to Georgia? They moved too much as it was. They were happy where they were and so was I. I couldn't keep moving these kids back and forth like this. Summer was finishing up college and the other two were about to go back to school. It was a mess all right. I signed the paperwork and walked outside in tears, not knowing what to do at all. I waited to call Mrs. Lisa to pick me up. I had to sit and ponder on this for a while. I sat outside the probation office for at least two hours. I didn't want to call the kids yet or my mom, so I called Ryan. I told him what they said and he was so helpful.

He gave me so many words of encouragement and told me to look at it in a positive light, like maybe I had unfinished business in Georgia success-wise. He said that maybe I left too soon before God could give me what he had in store for me. He said I could also try something where the kids could stay in Florida, go to school, keep working my account at night to pay the bills and I bring the babies down with me and stay with Mrs. Lisa until I was accepted by Florida. It just felt like nothing was possible at this point in my mind. I mean Ryan was so helpful, he stopped my crying session, but my life and my kids' lives were about to go on another merry-go-round. I thanked him for talking to me, we hung up, and I called and talked to my mom and told her. She was upset, so I tried some of the words on her that Ryan displayed on me to make her feel better. It worked a little, but she made the decision to get on the next flight and go to my house and stay for however long it was going to take after my week was up to come back to Florida to live for good. Then I hung up with her and called the kids. I did the same thing to them. I threw Ryan's words on them to try to encourage them and to my surprise, they were okay with it. They didn't mind coming back to Georgia. As I listened to myself use Ryan's words on my mother and the kids, the more it sunk in and their positivity about the situation helped me even more.

I finally called Mrs. Lisa to pick me up and within 20 minutes, she was there. I got in the car and she asked me what happened. I told her that I could go home for a week, but that I had to come back to live until I was accepted in Florida. Like me, she didn't feel that it was right either, but she stayed positive for me. She took me back to her house and I sat there in deep thought of how quickly my life got turned upside down. All I could do was what I knew best...pray. I prayed hard and I prayed long for God to turn my entire situation around in my favor. I let God know that only He could make such changes on my life and only Him. When I was done praying, I worried no more and just then my kids called me and said, "Mommy, we coming to get you." My cup runneth over. I was overjoyed. Since the girls couldn't drive, Tyrone and Marquez took turns and drove my truck with money from my mom and Summer's babysitting money for gas. What should have taken them six hours, took them 12. It seems they took a wrong turn and it took an extra six hours for them to get back on track. I couldn't wait to see them. All of them, which included Tyrone and Marquez. I loved those boys so much. They knew about my past situation and never judged me, they still called me mom. The twins were safe at home in Florida with my mom. It had to be around 1 or 2 o'clock in the morning when they finally arrived at Mrs. Lisa's house. We all did a great big group hug and kisses. I felt like it was more than three months that I haven't seen my kids. It was too long of being without them.

    They sat down and rested for a minute and told me funny stories about their travel and caught me up on some of the things that went on while I was gone. I missed my family so much, but being away from them for that long and just seeing them again, words could not express how my heart felt. My kids were my backbone. They were there for me, the whole nine yards and they absolutely loved me. Before it got much later, we started to hit the road after giving hugs and kisses and goodbyes to Mrs. Lisa and her family. I started out on the road and it felt like I haven't driven in years. I was more than ready to get back home. The boys and I took turns driving as it got later and later to morning hours. The money was getting extremely low for gas and God took us on home the rest of the way. I can't tell you what time it was exactly when we got into town, but I know it was bright, early daylight. Before we got to the house, we dropped the boys off at their houses and headed down the road a little further to our house. Home sweet home. I was really pulling up in my driveway, getting ready to go into my house. When I walked up the driveway, my baby girl LJ was looking out the window at me as if to say, "She looks familiar." Then I saw my little man, JJ. My heart broke in two. The babies began to realize that I was their mommy again and their eyes were just so huge staring at me, they couldn't take their eyes off me and they hugged me and would not let go. (Let me tell you, it is hard for me, at this actual second that I write this as I am taking myself back to that moment to continue writing this part). LJ looked at me and said, "Can we go to your house?" I told her, "baby, this is my house, we live here together, and it's our house." How could I ever leave those babies again?! The law said I only had one week to spend with them. What was I going to do?

Family Feud

Ephesians 6:1-2

Being back home was great. The twins slept with me the entire time I was home. Mother cooked everyday. I really missed her cooking. I called our pastor at that time, Pastor Duiwel who was helpful to the kids as well while I was gone. They explained to him why I was in jail and when they got into a tight spot, he helped them pay the electric bill. He was glad that I was home and he wanted me to come to the church to talk with him and his assistant, Brother Christopher, who was also a big help to us. When I arrived, they were just as happy to see me as I was to see them. We sat in Pastor Duiwel's office and talked for at least an hour while I explained the whole ordeal to them of why I was in jail in the first place and they were shocked at the fact that my own brother did something like this to me. I let Pastor know that I forgave my brother, but that I still needed a little more work in keeping that mindset, especially with my baby girl asking me if she could come to my house. My brother stripped me of my kids. Yes, I needed God and prayer to continue to be heavy in my everyday life.

Before I left, I made motion to pastor and Christopher that I was going to pay them back for helping the kids with the electric bill and they told me to not worry about it, because it was what they were there for. Pastor Duiwel proceeded with "we are family and if family needs, we shall provide for one another." After I left, I assured pastor that he would see us on Sunday. I went back home to my kids and my mom and took advantage of being in their presence.

Several days had gone by and my week was ending fast. Monday was quickly approaching and I had to be back in Georgia by 9AM that morning in the probation office. Not sure of exactly what I was going to do, I decided to wait until Sunday morning to officially place it all in God's hands. In the meantime, I continued to pray throughout my stay. At night, I would walk through my house and look in at each of my girls' in their bedrooms while they were asleep and say a prayer to God to not take me away from them. I thanked God for each of my girls and their uniqueness. They were sisters, true enough, but they were all different and each of them has many qualities that I love about them. I thanked God for their indifference and I thanked God for their love. I then went over to the twins, who were lying down with me on the couch because I gave my room up to my mother, and I thanked God for the twins existence. What was planned for one, I was blessed with two beautiful babies. I then went into another room with my Bible, got on my knees, and I had a talk with God just like I'm talking to you now and I told Him that I cannot be away from my family and our lives together another minute.

    I told Him that we needed each other and if He made it possible for me to not have to stay in Georgia that I would continue to praise Him and go to church. Sunday morning came and the kids and I got up ready for church. Just like I mentioned, I laid it all down on the alter in silent prayer and I surrendered all doubt, worry and concerns. I let it go...I just let it all go. After church, Tyrone and Marquez gave my truck the "once over" with checking the oil, water, and transmission fluid, along with my tires before I hit the road. I felt so confident enough and was going by pure faith that I knew I would be back. My family had the same faith, so Nevaeh went with me with the thought process of turning right back around.

    Nevaeh and I headed down the road to Georgia with nothing but faith. I had to come right back. I had no back up plan if I wasn't able to. God had to give me this. I couldn't see it being any other way. I couldn't make it in Georgia that was one of my main reasons for leaving and after I made the move to Florida, business fluctuated like never before; therefore I knew that moving to Florida was the right move for me in spite of Craig's mess. I planned to retire there. Right along the ocean waves I always said.

    We headed for Georgia taking the back roads. I called Mrs. Lisa to let her know that I was on my way back, but I didn't ask if we could stay there because I didn't want to burden her. I actually called a girlfriend of mine that lived in Gwinnett County.

    I told her that I was coming down for a few days and asked if Nevaeh and I could sleep at her house and she was like, "sure, just give me a call when you get into town." Well, long story short, we arrived into town, I called her, and she did not answer. Now this coming from someone that I let stay at my house for three days with her 20-something nephew instead of spending money on a hotel room. I thought it was too good to be true because she had just gotten a new boyfriend, so that had a lot to do with it. I didn't have enough money to get a hotel for Nevaeh and me, so we got something to eat and talked and laughed and slept in the truck in the parking lot of a hotel. When morning came, I drove to Wal-Mart where we cleaned ourselves up and changed clothes just before I headed to the probation office. I dropped Nevaeh off at Mrs. Lisa's then, not letting her know where we slept the night before. When I walked in that office, I had confidence and belief that I was going to turn back around. I continued to pray. I knew my God and He was not going to allow anyone to turn my life upside down anymore than they already had. I signed in and waited for my probation officer to call me to the back. I must have waited for at least 15-20 minutes before she called me back where I had to take a "mug shot" and they had to fingerprint me.

    After we did all that, she took me to the back and looked me up on the computer and said, "I'm shocked because your transfer came through, I don't understand how it came through so quickly." I told her, "God," she said, "You're right because this has never happened before." I knew then I had favor. I raced out of that office, zoomed to Mrs. Lisa's bursting with my news of what God did for me. We were so happy. I told Nevaeh, let's get back home. We gave our love to Mrs. Lisa and her family and headed back down the road. Nevaeh called home from my cell to let everyone know that we were on our way back. I was too happy. I couldn't wait to get back home to be with my family on a permanent basis again. Headed down the road, Nevaeh fell off to sleep and my mind drifted off with all kinds of thoughts of how I was going to thank God for the favor He's given me. I wanted to do more than just work and take care of my kids. I wanted to accomplish more for myself. So, of course, I planned on giving more of me to the church, continue my reading and studying my Bible. I would complete the cancer survivor book, then I had plans of incorporating my company and marketing myself better with materials of car magnets, flyers, etc., and making the company website even better with longing plans of obtaining an agent for my books. I had to work hard and even harder. I had a lot to do. I had a full plate and I haven't even gotten started yet. I didn't need any distractions. I felt like God gave me favor and a second chance for a reason and I wanted to show Him how grateful I was by doing more with my life and giving more of myself to Him.

Well, after we got home, I lost my job due to a lay-off. The same job that the girls were working to keep the house, car, and bills. I had to get on the grind fast. I had two weeks to find a job because I had one more paycheck coming from that lost job, but I made sure not to worry. I knew that God didn't bring me this far to turn away from me now. After all, I had favor. Within a week, I got another job in my field as a remote editor working from home. I was making $16 an hour and was paid on a bi-weekly basis. I worked Wednesday through Sunday 11PM to 9AM, so my mornings were free. My kids and I, along with Tyrone and Marquez, would take that time to go to the park to play basketball and tennis. This was something that we adopted on a daily basis throughout the week. Afterward, we would leave the park, make a quick run to the grocery store to get snacks and drinks and hit Blockbuster Video, but we could only rent a movie that we all agreed upon. I made the mistake before of renting a movie that turned out to be lame according to them because, in Marquez's words, "it was not a group decision." That was the rule; it had to be a "group decision." We spent so much family time together. My kids and I were inseparable from Tyrone and Marquez. We went everywhere together. The boys wouldn't leave my house until their curfew, which was 11 o'clock at night. If we didn't eat breakfast together, we certainly ate lunch and dinner. On Friday nights, Tyrone would come by with Marquez to pick the girls up for youth group at the church and on Sunday mornings, we met up at church. From there, we would make a date to meet up at our house later and go to the park to play basketball and tennis. Then hit up the grocery store, and grab a movie.

It was routine. Then a couple of kids from the youth group wanted to come over as well, but we were so close, we only let them come and stay for a little to hang out and watch a movie, but everything else, we kept sacred...that was our family fun time and we didn't want to share that with anyone. It was nothing for kids to be in and out of my house. I always made sure I had something for them to eat too. If I was low on food, I made do. I always shared. That was something I got honestly from my grandmother. She was the type of woman that she didn't care if you were a stranger, if you came to her house, she always fed you and at times, you would leave with a bag full of groceries. That's just how she was. God bless her soul.

After awhile, I started to get convictions from the Holy Spirit. I received them when I made good on one of my promises to God of reading and studying my Bible more. I had a closet large enough for me to use as a sanctuary where I would read, pray and talk to God and just meditate. I was being shown things within my household and within that church that wasn't right that I couldn't see before. I always take heed and act on convictions, so I decided to sit back and watch and pay more attention to my surroundings and the people around me.

Everything started coming to me more clearly after my mother went back to live with Daniel in Illinois. We had a deal that mom would live with me for six months at a time and with him for six months at a time, like when it was cold up there, she would be with me because Illinois cold weather was not good for her bones, as she has arthritis. I began to notice my eldest daughter and Tyrone getting closer rather than acting like mother, brother, sister family-type thing we had going on with Marquez and the other girls. She began to act distant and snappy. She was snappy to the point where I had to pop her in the mouth quite a few times. Then she started to talk like, "well Tyrone says this" and "Tyrone says that" as if he controlled her and he did.

I witnessed one afternoon where Tyrone came over to the house with one of the boys from youth group named Eddie. Eddie asked me if he could have something to eat and of course I told him to make himself a sandwich. Then Tyrone says out loud, "man I'm so hungry" so I told him, "Tyrone, if your hungry baby, go ahead and make yourself a sandwich." He repeated his words and did not move, but my eldest daughter did. She got up from the table and started making him a sandwich and gave it to him on a plate just for this lil' punk to look through the sandwich and ask, "Where is the lettuce?" My eldest daughter grabbed the plate and put on some lettuce and gave it back to him. He said, "where is the mayonnaise?" she got up again, grabbed the sandwich, and put on mayonnaise and gave it back to him, just for him to finger through it and look disappointed and from her looking at his face, the look on her face went from a smile to a frown. He made her feel like she didn't do a good job. My eyes couldn't believe what I saw. He controlled her. Then there was an incident where she began to have bruises on her arms and legs.

Now it was nothing for the kids to wrestle and they run to me with, "mommy look at what she did and mommy look at what he did," and Tyrone would have long scratches on his arms. I would say to my eldest daughter, "why you do that?" and we all would laugh, even her, but little did I know that Tyrone was really hitting her. What I thought was wrestling and what they portrayed to me as them horse playing was actually physical abuse. Then God started showing me where Tyrone's behavior was coming from: the pastor of that church. Everyone was talking about how Pastor Duiwel was bribing Tyrone with a little hooptie car, giving him a cell phone from his family plan, and putting him on his car insurance. All this was to ensure that Tyrone would always sing and play the piano in his church, which made the people come. Tyrone could sing and play the piano and Duiwel wanted to make sure he kept what he thought was a "gold mine." Tyrone's own sister was telling him to get away from that man, along with his stepfather and mother who referred to Duiwel as being "full of shit," but Tyrone didn't want to listen. He was a kid and he was given a car and cell phone and $150 a week to barely clean a church, of course, he was going to take the deal. Rumors had it that Duiwel was sexually abusing Tyrone, but nothing was actually done about it.

I began noticing Duiwel's attitude towards me and my family changing as well. None of us felt comfortable. My kids only wanted to go to that church on youth nights so they could mingle with their friends, but on Sundays, it was different. The ones that we used to interact with, especially the women, including Duiwel's wife would give us stares and looks that made us feel like we weren't wanted, which made us feel uncomfortable. I forbade my kids to go to that church ever again, including youth night.

Another source of Tyrone's attitude came from was his stepfather. The two of them did not get along at all. He never gave

JAILED BY BLOOD: INMATE 798175

Tyrone a key to the house and, at times, if he came home a minute passed curfew, he would lock him out of the house. His mother would side with the stepfather. One night, my eldest daughter came to me and told me what happened, so I let Tyrone sleep on my couch. It seems that his family went out of town to visit his sister and didn't even tell him until he made a phone call to either his mother or his sister. It was no problem and I trusted him at this point, at times, I even trusted him with my bankcard and pin number to get gas whenever he needed it because he had no money according to him.

After the other incidents began to occur, Tyrone seemed to have a problem looking me in the eyes and began wearing dark sunglasses when in the house and at night. His spirit in my presence felt different. Our spirits didn't mix at all. Something wasn't right and my daughter was the center of it I felt, so I had a talk with her and told her that something wasn't right with Tyrone because he stopped looking me in the eyes. I told her that I think something is going on or something is about to happen. She tried to convince me that he was fine and so was everything else and that she didn't see anything of what I was talking about. I decided to step back a little bit and I began to notice that he would come over to talk with only my daughter, but his attitude was always edgy and her moods were starting to become depressing. Her grades went from a 3.8 to 2.4. I would catch her crying and when asked what was wrong, she would lie and say there was nothing wrong with her; she was just sniffing, as if she had a cold or something, but she still had the snappiness in her voice. Tyrone didn't interact with all of us as much either, just her. As time went by, Tyrone was beginning to come around a little too much. I didn't feel like that before, but these visits didn't feel friendly at all, they were quite different from the others.

I would catch him and my daughter often times whispering to each other with a sense of "something not right was going on." I was getting fed up of Tyrone's appearances now. I told my daughter that he need not come over so much and that he really needed a job because half cleaning Duiwel's church for $150 a week was not enough. I told her that he needed a real job to occupy his time because I didn't want him sitting around my house all day til evening anymore. As soon as I said that, Tyrone's appearance was almost not at all, but when he did show up, he was even more distant. I couldn't help but to think that my daughter told him what I said so I confronted her and she swore up and down "mommy, I would never tell him something like that, it would hurt his feelings," come to find out, she actually did tell him. She told him everything that my other two daughters and I have ever said about him and then some. So when he did come around, he was completely distant and her attitude toward me and her siblings was ridiculous. She acted like she didn't want to be around us anymore. Living in my house was beginning to be unbearable for all of us, even for the twins because she would constantly yell at them instead of talking to them and if they ever called her name, she would ignore them and of course, being babies, they would cry and she would yell for them to shut up. If they would try to hug her, she would yell for them to get away from her by saying "move!" in a strong voice tone. She woke up with attitude and when I was in my room, my other daughters would tell me how she would argue with them and call them ho's and my oldest daughter, she would call a fat bitch. When I confronted her about it, she would try to loud talk and deny it all.

    I knew she was lying and that's why I popped her in the mouth. She began to have looks at me like she wanted to kill me. It was going from bad to worse and she was out of control, then one night, it all came to a head. The girls had a friend of theirs over the house. She was more of my eldest daughter's friend than she was the rest of them and I thought something strange because my daughter wanted to go to bed earlier than usual and she came in my bedroom giving me a big hug and a kiss on the cheek stating that she was so sleepy and tired and I remember thinking to myself, "now why is she going to bed so early when her friend is still here?"

    I went along with it and a few minutes later, I remembered that she had kitchen duty that night and I went in her room to remind her to sweep the kitchen floor. She had her room door cracked and when I opened it, she was not in her bed. I turned on her light and I looked in her closet and she wasn't there either so I went to the bathroom and nothing. So I went into my room and asked my youngest and their friend if she came back into my room because she was not in hers and they both said no. I went back into her room and pulled back her curtain and the window was open. I was fed up. I then took the little girlfriend home and informed my youngest to not open the door for her if she came back, but to only open it for my oldest because she was out babysitting at the time. When I got back, there she was sitting on the porch looking "busted."

I walked passed her and talked to her at the door and told her that I am not playing any games with her, either she was in or she was out and she started talking to me like I wasn't her mom. She said, "I'm leaving and don't be calling no cops either" and starting walking with a stank behind switch and a different outfit on of a very short miniskirt. I slammed the door and I did call the cops because she was a minor and I was still responsible for her being out there in the street.

When the police arrived, they wrote her up as being a runaway and I told them where I thought she might be and they followed me over to Tyrone's parents house. He was not there, they didn't even know where he was *(turns out he was sleeping in the church because he was kicked out of his house again)* and my daughter was with a neighborhood friend's house. They drove around to where the police and I were to Tyrone's house. She was sitting in the passenger seat of the friends' mother's car and the mother came up to me to let me know that my daughter had gone to her house and she suggested that I allow her to stay the night with her and she would bring her back home in the morning. I agreed and went home. I then called the pastors of our new church. Pastor Ken and Co-Pastor Tina of Heaven Ministries. They made plans to come over the next day to try to talk with my daughter and Pastor Ken made known that he wanted Tyrone to be there as well.

Morning came and I saw the break of dawn. My thought process was all over the place. I remember thinking how could this have happened? Maybe I should have been a little stricter with Tyrone and Marquez coming over or maybe I should not have been so friendly to them. I really didn't know how to feel. I think every mother goes through the same thing of blaming herself, however, I knew I was doing the right thing in regards to keeping them away from that church because something in my spirit was not settling with that pastor, especially when I later heard several rumors about him of trying to rape two young girls on separate occasions that went to school with my eldest daughter and the other was a friend of my oldest daughter. No charges were ever filed, however.

Noon came and so did Pastor and Co-Pastor Tina. About an hour later, my daughter and our friend's mother arrived to the house. We all sat around the table and my daughter just reeked with attitude. It was in her walk, her face, and in her words. She was so angry and to be honest, I don't even think she knew why. Pastor started the conversation off with telling us we all needed to learn how to communicate better, which he was correct in every way and all you could hear was my daughter mumbling something under her breath. Pastor then asked her if there was something she wanted to say or if there was something she wanted me to know. She began with she felt like I didn't understand what she was going through and before she wanted to say more, but she stopped herself for a lack of words and I told Pastor that I did understand, but it didn't mean that she was allowed to disrespect me in anyway and she mumbled again. I told Pastor, "see what I mean?" and I told him that when she talks back like that, it makes me want to smack her in the mouth and she blurted out with, "yeah, come on if you want to, I'll put you back to where you just came from," suggesting that she was going to put me back in jail. Pastor took her out of the house because I threatened to come across the table on her. (Can you believe that? She stated she was going to put me back in jail, knowing what I had just gone through with my own brother, now I had to watch my back from my own child. This wasn't the first time she mentioned about putting me in jail either. She mentioned it one day when we were out with our pastors handing out fliers to neighborhoods about the church. She was in the back talking about how she was planning to put me back in jail and Pastor Ken overheard her and told her to be nice).

Later that night, the tension began to ease up as Pastor Ken had a long talk with her on their walk and Co-Pastor Tina prayed with me and our other daughters in a prayer chain. It made for a smoother evening-- until they left. Her attitude came right back. She walked out of the kitchen into her bedroom and began to gather some clothes and we began a tug-of-war with them. I took most of her clothes and placed them into my closet. I told her that if she planned on leaving again, she was not going to take anything that I bought her and out of her mouth went, "you didn't buy these sweetie!" I popped her right in her mouth for talking to me like that and if looks could kill, she would have not have hesitated to kill me that very second. I looked her dead in her eyes and I saw nothing. She was not my child. It was like she wasn't even there, if you can understand that.

Later that night, I took the Bible and I went into her room to talk to her and I told her how much I loved her and the rights and wrongs according to God's Word and it was going in one ear and out the other because she was saying things like, "just let me leave" and mouthing off stating that she had something for me, but she couldn't tell me what, but I couldn't give up. I continued on and all of us gathered into the kitchen and I talked more until I felt like I got through to her. I told her that Tyrone was different than when we first met him. His attitude changed for the worse because Pastor Duiwel told him that he was going to get Tyrone his own apartment. The congregation was going to foot the bill, as Tyrone put it to us, and I heard through various kids in the neighborhood that Tyrone and my daughter were supposed to move in together and I couldn't allow that. I called Duiwel and told him what I heard and he wasn't at all interested in anything I was talking about, all he wanted to talk about was how Tyrone told him everything I said in regards to Duiwel bribing him and how he was mad that he gave us a free turkey for Thanksgiving, though he gave away turkeys to everyone in the congregation. He mentioned that turkey twice, as if he was really upset about giving it to us, because Tyrone told him that I gave it away to someone in the projects, along with sidings. My kids and I told Duiwel that we didn't need the turkey in the first place. I interrupted him, stating that I was not calling about a turkey, but about Tyrone and my daughter of how they planned on moving in together if he got Tyrone the apartment and I wanted to prevent it and he blurted out, "oh now you need my help huh?" "Well Ms. Storm, I tell you what, don't ever call me again." He hung up. I called him back and he let his answering machine pick up. I left a message telling him that he was the very reason why I left that church because he was a conditional pastor and a real pastor was unconditional and that he was not feeding me spiritually, but I have that now with my new current pastor and I hung up. Tyrone told my daughter that according to Duiwel, I called him up cussing him and threatening him and she believed it.

At that moment, she broke down with snot and tears and apologized to me profusely and gave me the tightest hug and my other two girls joined in with the twins hugging our legs. She admitted to telling Tyrone everything. I said about of how he was changing for the worse and that he needed to get a real job. I told her that Duiwel was not going to get him his own place, that was another form of bribery, and that it was not appropriate. I said how he was not to be trusted anymore because he couldn't look me in the eyes and he would always wear dark sunglasses, even in the house and at night and she told me that he said, it was the other way around.

He was a liar and manipulator and I think that because things were not right in his house, he impinged upon her, his problems and misery loves company, so he convinced her that her home life was just as miserable when in reality it wasn't. We had a lot of love for each other in my household and other kids felt it too, especially Tyrone, which was why he hung around so much, besides wanting to be with my daughter. He confided in me that all his family ever did was eat and watch TV and that no one would do activities with him like we did with playing basketball, tennis, etc. Tyrone was eventually kicked out of his house and later on, my daughter started telling people that she and I did not get along and I was the reason why she was not at home because I kicked her out of the house, which was a total lie and as the ones she told this to got the opportunity to listen to her talk more, they knew she was lying. She tried to make me out to be this awful mother, as if she was the only one out of my five children to be treated differently. Eventually, all her lies surfaced and the truth came to light. She asked if she could talk to him for a second and I told her that I would allow it for a few minutes and then I would pick up the phone. She called him and asked him why he lied to her and his tone was so cocky, arrogant, and nonchalant, but she couldn't see that. He told her that he would never lie to her about anything and insinuated that I was the liar. I interrupted and told him that he was no good and he talked back to me like he didn't give a damn. I told him that I knew what his plans were about them moving in together and his words to me were, "I don't know what that little girls' plans are, but those are not my intentions." I played this back to my daughter and she just didn't believe me from the looks in her eyes. This little bastard had mind control over her.

    Needless to say, the phone call ended in a hang up from my side. For the rest of that night, she was not so talkative, but looked to be confused. She looked as if she didn't know what to believe or which way to go. I was completely drained. How could I compete with and convince my own child that I was not a liar when this boy controlled her. I was fighting a losing battle. I went into my little sanctuary of my bedroom closet and I got on my knees and I prayed til I fell asleep with my Bible in my hand. The next morning was a bit shaky. The house was full of tension. The day just felt shitty and it went by so fast.

    Usually, our house is full of laughs, but that day it was so blah. No one was really talking to each other and we were all doing our own thing, either one was watching TV by themselves, the others in their rooms and me and the twins in mine. Night came and it was on. All the kids and I were in the kitchen and one thing about me, when I'm upset, I start to clean, so I decided to do the dishes that were left in the sink. I looked at the dishes for a while first, and then I cleaned a glass, a plate, and then a knife. While I was wiping down the knife, I had my head down, contemplating just putting the rest of the dishes in the dishwasher, well that was all my daughter needed to see because in her mind, I was going to try an kill her with it. Why and how she would come up with something like that, I don't know. All I can think was that Tyrone put negative thoughts in her mind. My other kids and I agreed that he turned her against us because of the negative way she was treating us all. I heard her mumbling again walking away going into her room and I heard her say, "this is bullshit, this is bullshit!" I followed her and asked her what she said and I went to smack her in her mouth and she started blocking my hands, then I saw that she had already had a small duffle bag packed away in her closet and she began to dig for more clothes inside her clothes bin. I tried pulling the bin from out of her closet and the more I pulled, the more she pulled it back away from me. I told her that she was not taking anything that I bought her and she stated that while I was gone, she bought these clothes. She always made sure to throw in my face about me being in jail.

QUIET STORM

Then she came out of her mouth with, "you ain't nothing but a bitch anyway that's just why I hate your ass!" She was bouncing up and down like I was one of those schoolgirls or something waving her hands up in the air, trying me. At that time, knowing me so well, my oldest daughter gathered the twins and my youngest stepped in between us as if to hold me back because they knew I was going to snatch her up and I did just that. I reached around my daughter and grabbed little miss smart mouth by her shirt and pulled her to me, knocking my youngest out from between us and I started whaling on her, but she was fighting me back. Next thing you know, I heard the twins screaming and crying and then all the kids yelling, "Stop, stop!" trying to pull us apart. I yelled and told her that she was probably happy that I was in jail and she said that she cried for me everyday, but I found that hard to believe with her continuing to say that she had something for me and that she was planning to put me back in jail. I then started to hear the cries and yells of the twins again and I saw the look on their faces, they started to look into space with devastation and my twin baby girl was starting to shake while my son started withdrawing and wandering off like he separated himself from the reality that was going on in front of his innocent, beautiful brown eyes. I had to stop. We went from the bed to the floor fist fighting as if we were fighting people in the streets.

When I let up, she didn't stop with her mouth, she ran into the kitchen and grabbed the knife and said, "here, kill me now, you know you want to" then commenced to calling me all kinds of bitches and telling me how much she hated me and stated that Tyrone told her what a big liar I was and how he was there for her while I was gone. I asked her in the midst of her yelling, "What could he have done for you in three months that I didn't do in 17 years?" and she couldn't answer that of course, she blew off the question and continued to call me a bitch and a liar and said, "He told me you just used him anyway." Now people that know me know that I don't use anybody and I especially would not prey on using anyone's children. If I ever needed Tyrone to do anything for me, which would be to put oil in my truck for me or to take my oldest daughter to college and pick her up because I worked two accounts at home and I couldn't go up and down the highway and watch the twins, it was taking too much time out of my work schedule, so I paid him $40 a week to take my daughter back and forth for me. Plus he was always at my house 24/7 eating whatever we ate. Remembering my kids' reactions to us fighting in front of all of them and remembering her words of trying to put me in jail and having something for me, I just kept looking at her in her eyes while she said with such passion, "I hate you." She seemed to put emphasis on that word "hate." She dragged the "h" and looked me straight in my face. I knew that she wanted me to put my hands on her again so she could call the cops on me, so I flipped the script on her and remained calm and I asked God in my head to take over. I then picked up the phone and dialed 9-1-1. I reminded them of who I was from calling the night before and asked them to please remove her from my house because I couldn't handle her disrespect. Dispatch sent over three squad cars. When they got to the house, she immediately ran off at the mouth and told them that I tried to stab her with the knife and they looked at me for an explanation and I explained to them that I was contemplating on putting all the dishes in the dishwasher. I was already a two-time felon. I was not about to go to jail for life for stabbing my own kid for being a smart behind when all I had to do was kick her butt for being out of line. I wasn't stupid. I loved my kids and I was not about to go back to jail, especially for something like that.

    They asked her if she had somewhere to go for the night and she was still showing her behind and I didn't have to say anything, she showed them how unruly she was by continuing to disrespect me with, "yes, I got somewhere to go and I can't wait to get out of here" then she went to get more clothes and I tried to stop her, but the officer told me to let her go stating that she would be back. She began to taunt me, looking at me calling me sweetie and shaking her head with the neck roll, saying that she bought those clothes (*she didn't even have a job*). She then looked at my youngest and said, "bye, I love YOU!"

    She said it only to her and said nothing to my oldest, which made her burst into tears on the spot. I yelled and told her how wrong she was to do that and she said, "oh I didn't mean it, but my oldest had it with her behavior, her feelings were already torn up and she told her, "just go" and she walked off and said, "oh well." She had no remorse.

    After one of the police escorted her out, the others stuck around and talked to all of us and the one said, "She didn't need to be around the babies acting like that." He said he felt they weren't safe around her. The other officer chimed in and said, "mom, she's gonna get tired of sleeping on someone else's couch, don't worry she'll be back" and the other said, "yeah, McDonald's don't pay that well" and we all laughed. Then another one said that I should have taken the hinges off her bedroom door to leave her without a door to close and the other said he would have made her sleep in the hallway. They cheered us up and after they left, the girls and I sat in the living room and talked about what took place. We were all in disbelief. Twins still looked devastated so we tried to cheer them up and put in a cartoon movie. They would not leave my side. The babies slept with me that night and a few more nights. My twin baby girl kept saying that her sister yelled at mommy. All I could do was pray that God erase from their minds what took place. As time went by, they started to get better.

    We later found out that my daughter was staying with friends of ours that was less than five minutes from our house. I was having a hard time with it, but I knew that she could never come back into my house again. I didn't trust her with trying to put me in jail and especially when I found out that she was sneaking out the window on an almost daily basis where Tyrone would be waiting for her in his car. I didn't have a problem with my girls liking or having a crush on a boy or boys, I just didn't want them getting caught up with just one because that was where problems began. I would prefer that they dated boys, let me meet them and bring them around me, so I can get a feel of them before I was comfortable enough to let them take my girls out on a date. With no man being in my house, I had to be careful with my children and I do the best I can with all of them.

    As days went by, I decided to stay on top of my daughter, even though she was not in my house, but legally, I was still responsible for her, so I stayed in touch with the counselor at school and informed her that my daughter was no longer living in my house, however, I still wanted to be informed of her grades. She let me know that she dropped from an honor roll student to a failing student. She said that she needed a credit and a half to get out of the 12th grade, but the school has not seen her. My other girls was telling me, "mommy, forget her, she wanted to leave, it's not your fault, she don't care about us," but they didn't understand from a mother's point of view. She was still my baby out there and rather she knew it or not, she needed me. I just couldn't let her go. So instead of letting the girls know that I was still following up on her whereabouts and her well being, I decided to keep it to myself because it was upsetting them.

In the meantime, in passing, I would see my brother with different women where he would lay low in the passenger side while he let the women drive his car or he would be in their car on the passenger side. After we would make eye contact, it seemed to really piss him off I guess because he thought that I would get revenge on him by telling his wife, of which they were still residing together as a family. Seeing him again, I felt nothing. I wasn't upset as others expected me to be. I actually kind of felt sorry for him because his pain was greater than mine in order for him to do something like that to my children and me. All I could think about was how God was going to show him how wrong he was and out cheating on his wife only added onto his problems and he didn't even know it. I've learned to let God fight my battles and He did so to the point that where my brother tried to get me to lose everything, it all turned on him where he and his family were evicted again and had to stay with people within their church, he lost his job, and his car was later repossessed. He tried to get another one, but it broke down to the point of no repair. Then I started seeing his wife out with her kids only. This still continues to this day where they are never spotted together anymore. I just keep him in my prayers and keep it moving. Our relationship will forever be severed, however, I forgive him and I still love him. I just have to forgive and love him from a distance.

A few weeks had gone by and I received a knock on my door. It was my daughter, but she wasn't alone. She had Tyrone with her along with a police officer and I could hear her talking to the officer, telling him that I didn't want her to graduate from high school because I refused to give her a book she needed to turn in and while she was at my house, she wanted to get the rest of her clothes. I didn't open the door. I didn't want to deal with anymore drama from her. I rather her keep her distance at that time because she caused nothing but heartache in my house. I didn't want her crossing my doorstep again and to bring the police to my house along with Tyrone was over the top. I didn't appreciate that at all. They finally left after they realized I wasn't going to open the door. This went on for two days straight. I then talked to a few friends of mine and they suggested I give her what she was asking for that way she couldn't blame me for anything just like she was currently doing when things didn't go her way. Everything was "mommy's fault."

In the midst of when we were fist fighting and from out of nowhere, she yelled out that she was raped. My youngest daughter yelled for me to stop and said she was raped. I stopped and asked her when and who and she said that she didn't know who the man was, but it happened back in 2003/2004 when Donovan – the twins father – and I were together and we fell on hard times and we lived in a motel for a few months until we got back on our feet. Donovan and I had a show to do of poetry/spoken word. We had a venue called Spoken Word Poetry and we always told the kids to never, ever open the door because we had the key. Even if someone knocked on the door, never to answer because we would do a special knock and follow it up with using the key. My eldest decided that she didn't want to abide by the rule and she left out after her siblings went to sleep and in her words, she started drinking with some guys/men and she apparently got drunk and one of them raped her. I asked her why didn't she bring this to my attention back then and she didn't really give me an answer as to why she didn't, she just kept saying she didn't know why. I hugged her and asked her if she wanted to go to counseling about it and she said she was fine because Tyrone told her that she overcame it...to be honest, I was speechless. Later on that week, my youngest asked her why did she leave when Donovan and I told them never to leave and her response to that was, "I didn't want to be around ya'll." At the time, she was 14. I still don't know what to say about that, but she found a way to blame me for it.

I waited one morning to go over to the friends' house where she was residing (she referred to them as her family now) and I took over her other bin full of her clothes along with the book she needed to graduate. Then I did her one better and I placed in the bin, her birth certificate and social security card. She wasn't there unfortunately, but I dropped it off with the family.

Then one afternoon, my mechanic had an auto shop that was next door to Duiwel's church and I saw her with Tyrone. He didn't see me though, as he was sticking his head inside of the church van like he was cleaning it out. She then turned around and looked straight at me and immediately turned her back and totally ignored me. She didn't even come next door to say hi. I was heartbroken. I gave my truck to my mechanic friend so he could take a look at my brakes and I walked away so he wouldn't see me cry. She made me feel like my sacrifices for her and her siblings were all in vain. If she only knew. There were days when I didn't eat just so they could have enough to get full off of. I would psych myself out and exercised, repeating to myself that I needed to lose weight anyway. I just felt unappreciated. She turned against me because of a boy that cared nothing about her that everyone could plainly see and her peers told her that he was not the guy for her. To her, everyone was wrong and Tyrone was right. He could tell her that the earth was square and she would believe it. He could convince her that her eyes were actually purple and she would agree. Now I can sit here and write to you and tell you how hurt I was, but still to this day, words cannot describe the feeling I felt at that moment...unutterable. I gathered myself and talked to my friend about the brakes on my truck, scheduled for another day for him to fix them and went home. I took the back road so I could avoid getting more hurt by seeing more of them had I took the other route home. I spent the rest of that day and night very depressed and hid it from my kids with a smile on my face. That night when I went to bed, I couldn't even pray or go into my sanctuary. I just laid in bed and cried until I drifted off to sleep.

QUIET STORM

Revelation, Restoration, Relaxation

Isaiah 54:17

*T*wo days later, I received a visit from a sheriff, serving me with papers that were against me of a temporary protection order from Duiwel. It was dated for the same day I saw my daughter with a time stamp that was just an hour after I saw her. I thought then maybe that was why she snubbed me. I quickly reverted back to when she said that she "had something for me," but she stated that she couldn't tell me what and then there were her threats of "putting me back in jail." I immediately grew angry because I knew it was all bogus and BS. Duiwel wrote his reasons of why he felt he needed the order against me, which he stated, "that on January 8, 2008, at approximately 3 o'clock in the afternoon, I waited outside his church parking lot and waited for "someone" to come out and when they didn't, I went over to the church doors and shook them, trying to get in."

He even had on there that I worked at home and what type of company I had and what hours I worked narrowed down to the days of the week. I never told Duiwel what days and hours I worked. The only one that could have known that was my daughter. Rumors started circulating amongst the kids in the neighborhood that they supposedly had me on camera and I was told that my daughter was cosigning for Tyrone. She was actually backing him up with his lies of me being at the church that day and being on camera. I was highly upset because she knows me better than that. She knows I wouldn't do anything to jeopardize my family or compromise my freedom. I had no reason to go to that church to do anything.

By that time, I was well into my new church of Heaven Ministries going on two months. I didn't know what to do. I decided to go to where my daughter was staying to confront her about these false accusations, but she wasn't there. I talked to the son of the house instead because the dad was never home and the mom moved out to another state right after my daughter moved in. The son was very concerned about me being upset for having being put through this. He gave me a hug and apologized to me for having to deal with the situation. I thanked him and asked him to tell her to call me and if she doesn't call me, then I know that she had something to do with it. I never received a call from her that night or any other night. I went back home and I called Pastor Ken and I broke down as I was telling him about the order and he immediately ordered me to stop crying and have the belief that God has already fought my battle. "No weapon formed against me shall prosper," he said. He then said that he was going to appear with me when it came time for court.

After I hung up the phone with him, I felt confident and a known fact came to mind. On the day and very time that Duiwel said that I was at his church, the kids and I were actually with a realtor looking at property for my mother, who planned on moving here. I called the realtor to see if she would write me a statement of my whereabouts and she agreed. She even did me one better, she typed up on her company letterhead the exact date, which was January 8, 2008 at 3 p.m., she was showing me property and named exactly the property she was showing me and had the letter notarized. Then to cover myself even more, I back tracked that whole day and got letters from my youngest daughter's school of what time I called to inform them that I was going to pick her up from school and the time I actually arrived at the school, then my mechanic even wrote a letter for me that stated what time I showed up at his shop for him to fix my brakes. I had all three affidavits and I was ready and waiting for that court day. My oldest daughter volunteered to go with me as a witness to testify on my behalf because she was in the car also along with the other kids to view the property for my mother. Lady Tina even came along for moral support along with Pastor Ken. She was prepared to vouch for my character because Duiwel put in the order that I displayed violent behavior, reported to the police that I made a false report of one of his members kidnapping my daughter, and that I supposedly made threats to members of his church of having them "taken care of." I have no idea where he got that from, but we all knew that he was talking about Tyrone because he was the only one my daughter was with. In regards to that lie, I did file a police report when my daughter first left and I suggested that she was with Tyrone, but I never said he kidnapped her. The police filed the report as her being a runaway. Neither the police nor I ever mentioned the word kidnapped. It was obvious they were out to get me. Duiwel laid it on thicker by saying that I was currently on probation for a felony charge. He tried to make me sound real bad.

This is who my daughter continues to follow and proudly states that his church is her church and from what I was hearing, she was in this man's church every Sunday for service, every Thursday for Bible study, and every Friday for youth night and even hanging out helping Tyrone when he was supposed to be cleaning the church. She knew that Tyrone and Duiwel tried to put me in jail off of a lie and she still dealt with them. How messed up is that, but if she had a problem with someone, I am expected as a mother to defend her. Just like I did when one of their church members was speaking unpleasant about her in regards to her, in this member's words, "dressing like that to get Tyrone." She felt like my daughter dressed inappropriately to catch Tyrone's eye. When my daughter was very upset and brought this to me, I did what any other mother and/or family member would do to defend their family and I went up to that church and brought it to Duiwel's attention and he defended that woman to no end and stated that he never heard anything like that being mentioned, but my daughter told me that Duiwel was right there agreeing with the woman when she made that statement.

My daughter totally wrote me off and had no remorse in doing so. February 7, 2008 at 9AM, the court day came. Pastor and Co-Pastor Tina met my oldest daughter and me at the courthouse. While waiting to be taken inside the courthouse, we saw Tyrone and Duiwel sitting there looking the opposite way. I made it my business to keep looking them in their faces in hopes of catching their eye. I wanted them to look me in my eyes and they made sure they would not look my way. It was so obvious that they were avoiding looking at me and I know they knew I was looking at them. The sheriff came and opened the doors to the courtroom and we took our seats.

Pastor Ken called me out so we could talk and he take a look at the evidence that I had and gave me the advice to let Duiwel and Tyrone talk to the judge first, then afterward, I was to hit them with my evidence, which will have made them perjure themselves. We went back in and before the judge began any cases, he stated the penalty for perjury, which was five years of imprisonment and I saw Tyrone and Duiwel look at each other. After we heard a few cases that were presented before ours, maybe around almost two hours later, the bailiff called our case and we walked to the front and sat in the seats at the tables in front of the judge and Pastor Ken and my oldest daughter came to the front with me while Duiwel and Tyrone sat on the other side to the left of us. I sat down and opened up my folder and I was more than ready to present my evidence and I noticed Duiwel glancing over at me curious as to what kind of paperwork I had because neither one of them had any paperwork. I thought they had me on camera remember? Where was the video? They had absolutely nothing in their hands. When the judge told them to begin with their case, Duiwel stated that he wanted to drop the case because in his words, "she has not come back to the church since then." What a lying lil' punk. I couldn't wait to talk. When the judge looked over at me and stated that the plaintiff wished to drop it, I told him that I really didn't want to because I was ready to present my evidence, but the judge looked like he was already irritated and asked Pastor Ken who he was and he told him that he was my pastor and the judge asked if he could help out because he felt like we needed some "spiritual guidance" right now. Pastor Ken then looked at me and said, "Storm, just let it go right now." He read the look on my face of wanting to hang those niggas and he said, "I know, it's already taken care of, so just let it go." I agreed and told the judge that it was okay with me. I was pissed, especially when I heard Duiwel mumble under his breath, "everything is fine as long as she don't try to shake the doors again" and he and Tyrone laughed very low. The judge didn't hear his comment, but he did hear him say, "She is always welcome back to the church" because he made sure he spoke up and said it loud so everyone in the courtroom could hear it. He was nothing but a devil. I couldn't believe he got away with it, but my pastor told me that Duiwel and Tyrone didn't get away with anything. He said that God will punish Duiwel severely for being a man in his position lying the way he has and assured me that Tyrone was gonna get his as well. When we left out of there, none of them still couldn't look me in the face. They actually waited for us to walk out first then walked slowly behind us. Damn cowards.

QUIET STORM

    The next day, I received a "private call," it was my eldest daughter. I wanted to take this call when I heard her voice because it was important to me that she knew the truth and I show her my evidence because I knew those niggas told more lies about the turnout from court. She stated, "I called...well, I don't know why I called, but I wanted to call you." She asked me if I could pick her up around the corner, not wanting me to show up at the friends' house where she was staying. I agreed and took my paperwork of evidence with me and there she and the little girlfriend were in the middle of the street smiling at me. They got in the car and she immediately said, "I didn't know anything about what happened until afterward."
Just from that statement, I knew she was lying and the kids in the neighborhood were right about her backing Tyrone up with saying that I was at the church and they had me on camera. Plus, I know that the son told her I was there and gave her the message the first night I got the paperwork. At that moment, I felt more betrayed because she was actually in my face lying to me and lying with a straight face. Part of me wanted to smack the shit out of her and the half of me wanted to just walk away and never speak to her again. Instead, I just continued on with the conversation and told her that I had evidence and began showing it to her and the look on her face was as if she was shocked. Then she followed it up with, "I knew you wouldn't do anything like that." Yeah right...I just didn't believe her. My gift of discernment would not allow me to. She also told me that Tyrone and Duiwel did go back to the church and told everyone that they dropped the case and that Duiwel said that he didn't want me in his church ever again. She then asked if she could go to "my house" as she put it to see the twins and of course I did so.

    We went to the house and the kids were happy to see her. Her and my next to my youngest daughter started catching up on people and a little gossip until it was interrupted with a phone call to her cell phone from Tyrone. She was speaking to him as if she was in morris code or something. He must have asked her where she was because he was at the friends' house looking for her and she hesitated to tell him that she was with me at my house. When she hung up her cell phone, she was silent and immediately jumped up and put her shoes on in a quick hurry and uttered, "I have to go, uh, can you take us to the corner?" not to the house, but she wanted me to drop her off around the corner from the house. The way she was rushing out the door, I asked her if Tyrone hits her and she was silent, so I asked again and she just looked at me without any words and many minutes later said, "uh no, not anymore." My blood was boiling. This little bastard was actually putting his hands on my child as if he had the right.

After I took them to the corner, the little friend got out of the car after saying goodbye to me and my daughter looked at me and held me so tightly and just kissed me all over my face and told me she loved me and just then, Tyrone pulled up with piercing eyes straight at her and she looked as if she was a little kid who just got caught doing something she wasn't supposed to because her eyes got so huge with fear. When I saw the look in her eyes, I turned toward him and looked him dead in his face and he would not look at me, he tried to play it off and said to her, "man, I been looking all over for you cuz" he said it twice trying to say it in a funny way, but you could hear the anger in his voice. What an asshole. She got in his car and I did not hear from her or see her for at least a month and I couldn't call her because the last time she called the house, she called with the number blocked.

Several months had gone by and I still haven't heard anything from her. I started hearing stories about her being in constant arguments with Tyrone; they must have broken up a million times. Seems that Tyrone's little lies about him getting his own place via Duiwel were coming to surface. He ended up living with a church member of Duiwel's. (Still to this day and continuing to half clean the church for $150 a week, no other occupation or college goals). I was hearing rumors of him still putting his hands on her and she being in fistfights with girls over Tyrone, thinking someone wanted to date him. He even took her to one of the young girls homes that went to their church just so she could fistfight her, which ended up in my daughters arrest for aggravated assault. She spent a few days in jail until the judge let her out on her own recognizance. I tried getting in touch with her but she didn't want me to. It was obvious, so I started telling her friends to send her the message that I loved her and I missed her. I never got a response back. Soon after, I began adopting the attitude that everyone told me of letting her go. Continue to pray for her and put her in God's hands. Let go and let God is what I began doing. I got on with my life and I was having a ball. I felt free and like a burden was lifted. Months and months went by and the more blessings I was receiving. We were attending church every Sunday with Pastor Ken and having Bible study at our house every Wednesday. I even obtained a second account with a company in Texas as an auditor making $15.00 an hour Monday thru Friday. Life was great. I was clocking approximately $60,000 per year by myself and enjoying life with my kids to no end. I had my fines and fees paid up and I was working on obtaining a literary agent. Life got much better once I let go. Later on, we started seeing my eldest daughter in passing like in Tyrone's car and she wouldn't acknowledge us. No one blew the horn, but we could see her look over at us and not even give us a wave or smile, but she managed to look evil. Several times we saw her with the friend's family at Wal-Mart and we just kept walking. I just didn't care anymore. I was over it. She made me feel like she didn't love or care anything about me, and that she really did hate me because that was exactly what she showed me, but I had four other kids that adored me and I was content.

As time went on, the kids and I were living our lives in high spirits and enjoying each other. I started thinking along the lines of having a new start. Everybody knew where we lived and I wanted to move out of that house. Just leave all that baggage of old memories and start off fresh and what better to do it along with my new attitude than a new home. I stayed in constant prayer about it and the plus was that I was on a month-to-month lease with the real estate company. It was just a matter of finding something decent along with a nice neighborhood and what comes with a nice neighborhood of manicured lawns and beautiful house is the right price that I could afford. I informed the real estate company that I planned on moving.

They were not too happy, but it was a good thing that I did move forward because a messenger from the bank that financed the house I was living was up for foreclosure. The man placed a folded over letter on the door and walked away. I read the letter and it seems that the owners were taking the rent I was paying them for the last two months was being put in their pockets instead of toward the mortgage. The letter was stating that the owners were in default of their loan by well over $2000 and if they did not pay for the current month by a certain date, then the proceedings for foreclosure was going to take place.

I looked at that letter as a blessing, giving me a heads up. At that split second, I decided that the real estate company and the owners was not going to see anymore rent from me. My kids and I did not hesitate to start packing up knick-knacks and what-nots. We began to drive around looking for rentals and started looking up houses on the Internet. I informed my probation officer of what was going on and being as sweet as she is, she let me know what areas she covered, that way she would still be my probation officer and not someone else if I moved out of the way of certain areas. I made sure to look within her perimeters. I found a home that really struck my interest after coming across a few not big enough, too small, don't really like the neighborhood, rent too high, and most did not have what I wanted of a separate living room, dining room, and family room. This house was in a new development that looked like it was a gated-community. The houses were beautiful with a lake view in your back yard, as well as a lake view in your front yard and it was in a cul-de-sac.

Perfect! My oldest daughter and I met with the landlord and she gave us a tour of the inside and it had exactly what I was looking for with a separate living room, dining room, and family room. It was only a three-bedroom and two-bathroom home, and the price was about $25 more than what I was used to paying, but for what I was getting of the lake views and cul-de-sac, new development and community, that extra $25 was well worth it. She asked me if I liked it and I told her that I loved it. She said that she would let her husband know and that he would give me a call later that evening to "seal the deal." I had my digital camera with me to take pictures of the house to show my youngest daughter after she got home from school and to upload onto the computer to email the pictures to my mother. We all fell in love with the house. I waited patiently for the phone call, trying not to be too anxious and the phone rang. It was the husband and he stated that his wife thought that I was a sweetheart and because of that statement from her is what made him really call me. He said that she really liked me and knew that I was the perfect tenant for the house because when she was showing it to me, I asked her if we should take off our shoes before we walked onto the carpet. Then he began to be fairly blunt with me and came right out and asked if I could afford the house and I told him that I had no problems with paying rent and I had no problems with paying the rent on time.

I assured him that I was secure with my career and he then gave me directions to meet him and see his wife again at their home to sign the lease and put down the security deposit and first month's rent. I was ready because I held back the current months of rent from where we were and I got paid the next day to cover everything else. All was falling into place so smoothly. I couldn't believe it. I was overjoyed and I could not stop thanking God for blessing me. I fell asleep thanking Him.

The next day, I followed my directions carefully to my new landlord's home and they informed me that their very close friends were actually the owners of the house and that after the year lease was up, that they would lock in the price with a two-year lease signing and I had hopes of possible purchase in the near future. Then they did me a deal even sweeter and made the rent due on the 15th of each month. Can't get any better than that. This made it so much easier on me because you know how bills can be when they are all due at the beginning of the month. I couldn't move quickly enough. After we signed the lease, I got into my truck and thank the Lord some more. I went home and immediately starting calling around pricing moving companies. I informed the real estate company where I currently was and told them that I would officially be moving out by the end of the month, which was by then less than two weeks.

The owners of our previous home asked me about paying for the current months rent and I told them about the letter that was left in the door. They totally lied to me and said that there was no such foreclosure and that they were never late with the mortgage, but I knew what I read and I refused to give them a penny. There really wasn't much they could do because they knew the truth about the house being up for foreclosure, plus I was on a month-to-month lease. They just tried to bully money out of me, but it was not going to work. I went ahead with my plans and my kids and I continued to pack the house up to get it ready for the movers.

As we were packing, my girls told me things they witnessed about my eldest daughter acting a fool of how she would verbally abuse and constantly fistfight my oldest daughter and would stop working on the account and shift she was assigned to and in regards to her room, they said that live frogs would somehow come out of her closet and that she always complained about black spiders biting her. She was killing a spider almost every night. Spiders and frogs were in her room only, never in any of ours. I talked to Tina about it and she told me that those creatures represented witchcraft, then she asked me if my daughter has ever dabbled in witchcraft before and I honestly did not know if she had or not. Sad to say, I felt like I didn't know my daughter at all. When I look back at when my kids were growing up, she was always the one that gave me trouble. She was the one that got the belt and at times, my hand to her mouth for speaking to me wrong. I just didn't understand how you can raise all your children the same way under one roof and one turns out the opposite of what you taught.

Tina told me that the foreclosure was God's way of taking us out of that old house and that I was on a path to a new beginning, especially with leaving all the emotional baggage behind. However, she disturbed my spirit when she said that while I was in jail, the enemy was attacking my daughter. She said that the best thing I could do for my daughter at this point was to give her to God and let God deal with her, then she reminded me of the scripture.

Ephesians 6:1-3 "Children obey your parents in the Lord for this is right. Honour thy father and mother; which is the first commandment with promise; that it may be well with thee, and thou mayest live long on the earth."

Tina stated that my daughter was actually hurting herself in shortening her days on this earth by being disobedient. She suggested I allow God to work on her. God was not nearly through with her yet. This was just the beginning. We must have stayed on the phone for at least two hours from a midnight phone call. I believed what Co-Pastor Tina said, I trusted her, and I did exactly what she suggested. I moved on and kept focus on my other kids. We moved into the beautiful house and I couldn't feel more at home. I felt like the house was made just for me. I was so comfortable and I would walk through the house at night and take it all in with a little glass of wine for a night cap. I enjoyed every corner of the house. As time went on and life was going so well, I decided to incorporate my business of Mallory Auditing Service and make it an LLC. I obtained permission from the owners to operate my business out of the house and abided by every rule of the state of Florida.

    I felt like there was more for me to do so I took that route and to me, I felt like I was showing God how much I appreciated Him for everything that He has done for me by not being at a stand still and settling. I began to move forward and really put my all into my book writing and promoting myself by inquiring into book signings where my books were sold at Barnes and Noble, Borders, and Books-A-Million. I began marketing myself even more by advertising car door magnets to go on each side of my blazer with my company information. I received a lot of inquiries about my business and have been approached by several potential clients. I even sent emails to talk shows and black magazines to try to get an interview and/or article. Life was going well. My oldest daughter began working full time while completing her Bachelors online in Graphic Design and moved out and into a three-bedroom, two-bath nice duplex for herself. She was less than five minutes away.

    Even though everything began falling into place, I couldn't help but to think about my eldest daughter and how I wanted her to come home so she could leave out the right way like her big sister. I knew that if she stayed out there long enough, she would not have the desire to do anything more than what she was already doing, which was hanging out by going to the clubs, drinking, smoking, house parties, not going to school, but working part time, however, not accomplishing anything. She was throwing her life away and I couldn't allow that to happen. I decided to call the school and I spoke with her counselor and she informed me that according to the attendance record, my daughter was not in school for weeks at a time. She stated that she needed an English credit to receive her high school diploma. I couldn't allow her to mess herself up like that, so I made up my mind to drive myself over to where she was residing and I talked to her. She seemed happy to see me, especially with the tight hugs she would give.

    I told her what her counselor told me about getting that credit in English in order to receive her diploma and she said that she would go to the school and register for summer school, but I didn't believe her so I did it for her and the counselor allowed me to sign her name on her behalf since I am her mother and neither the counselor or myself wanted to see my daughter get that far in school just to not get her diploma when needing only one credit. I signed the paperwork and she was all set to go. I then went back to that house and I gave my daughter a copy of the paperwork, which read that she had to be at the school as early as 7AM. She stated that she had a ride there, but was not too sure of a ride home. I, of course, offered, which also meant that by taking her home that would allow me to know that she actually attended. The way that the course went you could obtain your diploma at your own pace for instance, if it took you a week, then you would get your diploma in a week or if it took you a month, then you would get your diploma in a month. After about a week's time, my daughter received her high school diploma. I sent her a text message and asked her if she was hungry and of course, she said yes and I told her to be ready in five, which was the amount of time it took me to get to her house. She came out the door smiling from ear to ear and showed me her diploma then asked me if I wanted it. I was ecstatic. (Of course, I wanted that damn diploma, I worked hard for it!). She then thanked me for pushing her to get it because she stated that she was not going to go back. I wanted to talk to her about college, but decided to take baby steps because we just started communicating and the situation was delicate, so I was careful of my words because although she thought that she was "grown" she was still very much a young teenaged child. We had a good breakfast and nice visit and later on that day, I dropped her off and went home feeling accomplished. I immediately put her diploma up on the shelf next to her picture inside of a glass curio along side her older sister's diploma and picture. I started getting phone calls from my daughter now, asking if I would come to pick her up so she can spend time with us. She liked doing that when she was off work. I never turned her down. It was like old times, as she would lay in my bed, snug underneath the covers and watch a movie with us with a bowl of chips and soda. I let her know that she could come home anytime she wanted to, but she would always just say okay in return, not giving any hint that she wanted to or not. I knew that she was still seeing Tyrone, but barely going to Duiwel's church.

    My daughter coming over to spend time with us became more and more often. I even began taking her to work and picking her up at times when she was unable to obtain a ride. The more she was at my house, I believe she felt the love that she was missing and made mention to my youngest daughter that she wanted to "live in my house," but looked at it like it was a hard decision for her to make because she was still dealing with Tyrone and she knew how I felt about him, especially with not allowing him to come anywhere near my house, then she was so used to hanging out all hours of the night and she knew I wasn't having it. I assumed the nightlife and Tyrone took over her brain because she was still out there for quite some time.

It was months and months after we started communicating that she actually asked if she could come back home. It seems that the young lady whose house she was in was stealing money from my daughter and my daughter felt like she was set up by this young lady by not helping her out in a fight she had at a house party that was infested with a girl gang that planned on hurting her that night. The girl gang jumped her and her and the young lady fell out because of that. It was that night, I received a call from my daughter asking me if she could come home, but in her words, "can I stay with ya'll for a little while?" I asked her what was "a little while?" and she replied with, "I don't know, two months or so." I asked her what was she going to do after two months and she stated that she didn't know. I informed her that I have rules and she would have a curfew and she agreed to it. An hour later, she was driven to my house by a friend of hers. I showed her to her room, which was my exercise/workout room where I had to remove all my equipment and place it in the garage, setup as my new working out area and I set her bed up that was catching dust in the garage.

The next morning, I took just her and myself out to breakfast because I wanted to talk to her about the rules and curfew and I wanted to see where her head was at as far as her goals in life. We sat down eating our breakfast and before I could began to talk; she interrupted me with, "wait, before you start, I want you to know that I don't plan on living with my mom forever." I told her, "Momma don't plan on any of you living with me forever." I told her, "my job was to get her to achieve her high school diploma, now my other job is to get you the hell out my house." We both laughed. I wanted her to start off on the right foot with obtaining a roommate first before seeking her own first place. I asked her if she had any plans for college and she stated that she desired to attend college online for a social worker and to go as far as receiving a Masters. That sounded good and I let her know that we could get started on that soon enough, like that following week. She also let me know that she and Tyrone were no longer a couple, but they were just friends and that she was interested in someone else.

    I didn't really indulge too much in that conversation, in regards to Tyrone, but I did let her know that he was to not come anywhere near my house or to even ever call my house. Deep down I was still a little upset that she would still even consider communicating with him after what he and Duiwel tried to do to me, but I didn't mention anything about it. I interrupted with letting her know that she had a midnight curfew and that she would be back on taking turns with my youngest daughter of having kitchen duty and just chores in general. I could see that God was still working with her because throughout the recent communication, I could still see attitude and it really showed when I mentioned the time of her curfew. As weeks went by, there has been a few incidents where it has been a little bumpy for her trying to adjust back to "mommy's rules" and she was missing curfew by 30 minutes and at times, an hour or two from hanging out smoking black and milds, drinking illegally, and clubbing. A few times, I refused to open the door because she was past curfew. I wanted to let her know that she was not to take my kindness for a weakness. I also gave her a timeframe for after Christmas so I can make sure I have a good New Year. I didn't want to deal with anymore nonsense or stress in my house, so I believe three months from now was a good time frame for her to get herself together and I made her pay me $50 per week from her paycheck *(she gets paid on a weekly basis)* and I put back $25 towards a little nest egg for herself for when she moves out to be on her own. I was not going to be passive like I used to be with her.

    She still has a ways to go yet and God is still working with her, as He is with all of us, no one is perfect. The following week, my oldest daughter came over and helped us out with FAFSA and school paperwork to get the ball rolling on taking classes online. I reminded my eldest daughter that I don't raise lazy children that didn't want to do anything with their lives. I don't settle, therefore, my children will be taught not to settle. Ambition and determination is the word in my house. Every now and then, she needed a kick in the butt, but she knows that this go round, momma ain't playing. My youngest began her first year of high school and she is just a great big ball of anxiety to the point where she cannot wait to go back to school the next day. She loved high school. She already started out with having a great freshman year by meeting up with all her friends from the middle school last year. I believe the remainder of her high school years will be just as exciting as her first day. The twins began pre kindergarten, learning from the Abeka Curriculum, which entails religion in all the teachings. They come home singing Jesus songs and they learned how to spell their names. When my youngest and the twins began school, I think we must have snapped a thousand pictures for the first two weeks. I would upload them and email them to friends and family.

In the meantime, my writing career began making progress. I decided to put more time into my writing and spending more quality time with my kids, which meant that I had to let the night account go. I kept my morning one that was less stressful. On my lunch breaks, I promoted myself more, which ultimately led me to obtaining an agent.

My very first book, that I wrote several years ago, was pitched to my agent and she loved it. The plan is to now pitch the book to a producer to turn it into a movie on Lifetime. While that is in the works, I have book signings set up for all the books and even been on live radio for the cancer survivor book I wrote that ranged in autobiographies that I turned into chapters of diversity with an age range of 13 to 65, cancer survivors from all over the United States and some of the inmates. Now, my main goal for this book is to make an appearance on a television talk show to share my story. I practice what I preach to my children, "never settle, ambition, and determination is the key." As I take a glance back at the traumatic experience that has taken place in my life, I still cannot digest the fact that I was sitting behind bars not knowing exactly when I was going to go home. It has been approximately a year and some months now and I still keep in touch with several former inmates with phone calls and letters, planning to meet up in Miami at a hot poetry spot to watch me complete a performance I gave briefly on my way out the cage.

JAILED BY BLOOD: INMATE 798175

    Later, I would hear from kids in the neighborhood that Tyrone stated "he doesn't have anything bad to say about me or my children" and that "he even had a dream about he and I talking and laughing together like we used to." I really have nothing to say about that, except that I feel absolutely nothing towards him. No animosity, however, no desire to ever speak to him again either.

    In passing, I would still see my brother Craig. He would never look me in the face and, if by accident, he would catch my eye, he would quickly turn away. I assume from him being ashamed. I don't hate my brothers or my dad. I forgive all of them and I can truly speak those words and feel it without having any mixed up feelings about it. I do forgive them, however, I forgive them from a distance, as I am convinced our relationship is completely severed, and although my daughter has never said, "mommy, I'm sorry," I am at peace and eternally grateful to God for carrying me throughout my revelation, which led me to restoration, and now, I can finally have relaxation...

FALSE ACCUSATIONS

JAILED BY BLOOD: INMATE 798175

IN THE CIRCUIT COURT OF THE
IN AND FOR ▇▇▇▇ Seventh ▇▇▇ COUNTY ▇▇▇ JUDICIAL CIRCUIT,

Case No.:
Division:

▇▇▇▇▇▇, Petitioner,
and
▇▇▇▇▇▇, Respondent.

PETITION FOR INJUNCTION FOR PROTECTION AGAINST ▇▇▇▇

I, ▇▇▇▇ *(full legal name)*, the following statements ▇▇▇

5. Other prior incidents (including dates and location) are described below:
   On *(date)* 01/8/08 (Tuesday) at *(location)* ▇▇▇▇
   Respondent came over to the Church (about 3pm) and parked at car park waiting for some to come into the building. after waiting for a while without any body showing up she went and forcefully try to shake the church front door open.

   ☐ Check here if you are attaching additional pages to continue these facts.

6. Petitioner genuinely fears repeat violence by Respondent. Explain: ▇▇▇▇ has behaved hysterically lately, calling police to the house of one of our members to make false claim of kidnapping, she has threatened to send ppl to "TAKE CARE" of one of our members. She has called us on the phone using profane words added to the fact that she is a convicted felon on probation rightnow. We can not take chances and totally unsure what next step she is going to take. She has proof to us countless times that she cannot be trusted.

7. Additional Information
   [✓ all that apply]
   ___ a. Respondent owns, has, and/or is known to have guns or other weapons.
   Describe weapon(s): Not Sure

   ___ b. This or prior acts of repeat violence have been previously reported to: *(person or agency)*
   No

SECTION IV. INJUNCTION (This section must be completed.)

Florida Supreme Court Approved Family Law Form 12.980(f), Petition for Injunction for Protection Against Repeat Violence (03/04)

MY PROOF
JAILED BY BLOOD: INMATE 798175

**Albert M. Esposito
&Associates, Inc.**
Licensed Real Estate Broker

February 6, 2008

To whom it may concern:

This will certify that I was with ▇▇▇▇▇▇▇ showing her property at 3 P.M. on January 8, 2008 at ▇▇▇▇▇▇▇▇▇▇▇▇▇▇▇▇

Very truly yours,

Nancy E. White

Nancy C. White

State of Florida
County of Flagler

This document was acknowledged before me on ~~January 6~~, February 6, 2008 by Nancy C. White, who is personally known to me, and executed this document in my presence.

Brandy Reifsteck
Notary Public

Brandy Jo Reifsteck
Commission # DD431242
Expires May 19, 2009

386/439-5783 Office • 386/439-0082 Facsimile • Email: abesposito@bellsouth.net
326 Moody Boulevard • P.O. Box 1836 • Flagler Beach, FL 32156-1836

JAILED BY BLOOD: INMATE 798175

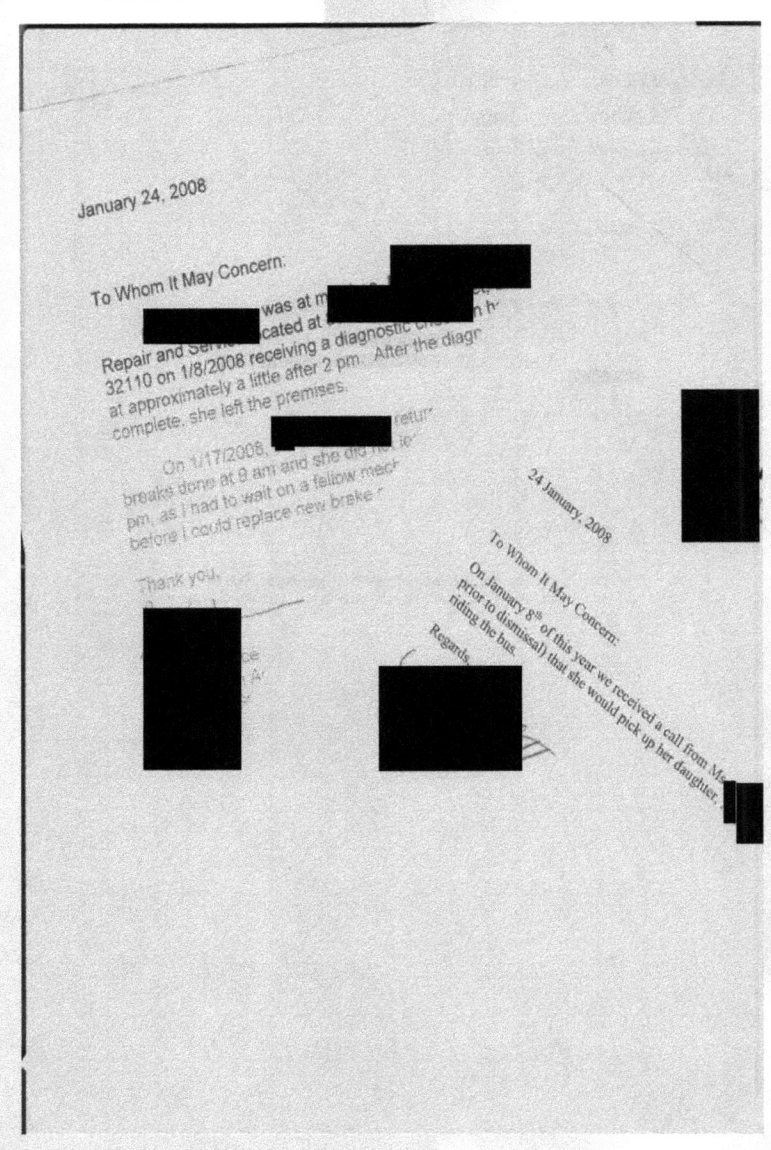

LETTERS FROM HOME

JAILED BY BLOOD: INMATE 798175

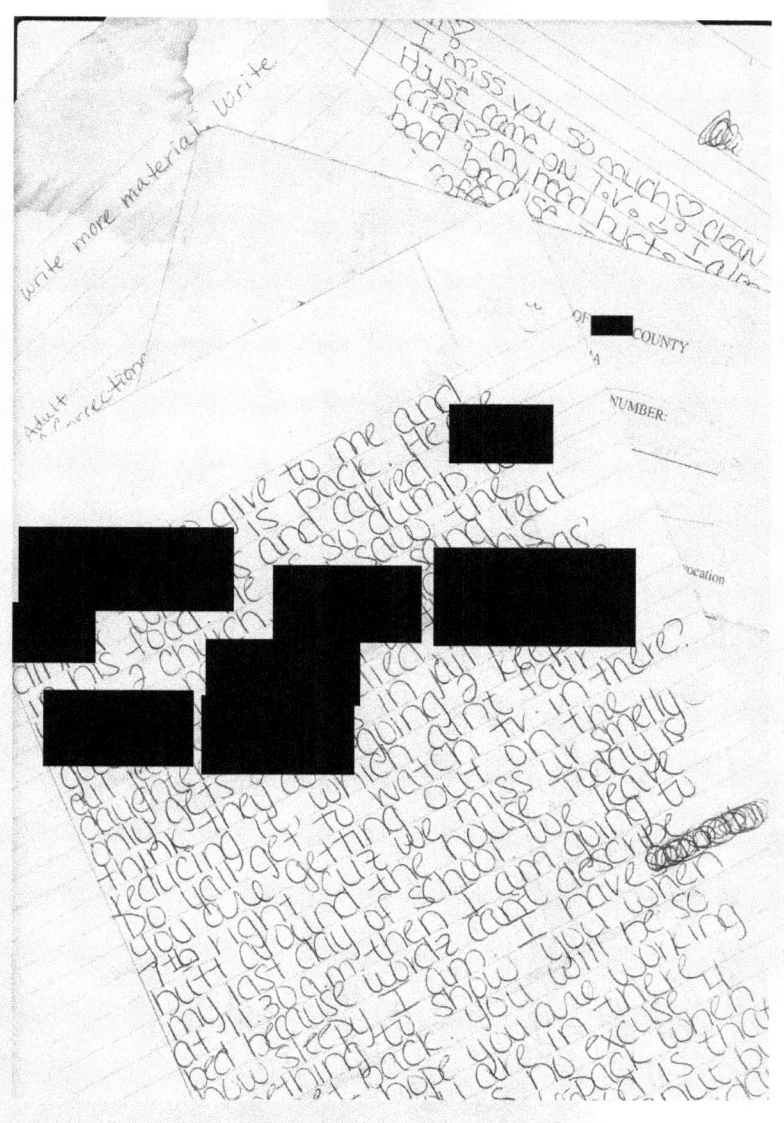

JAILED BY BLOOD: INMATE 798175

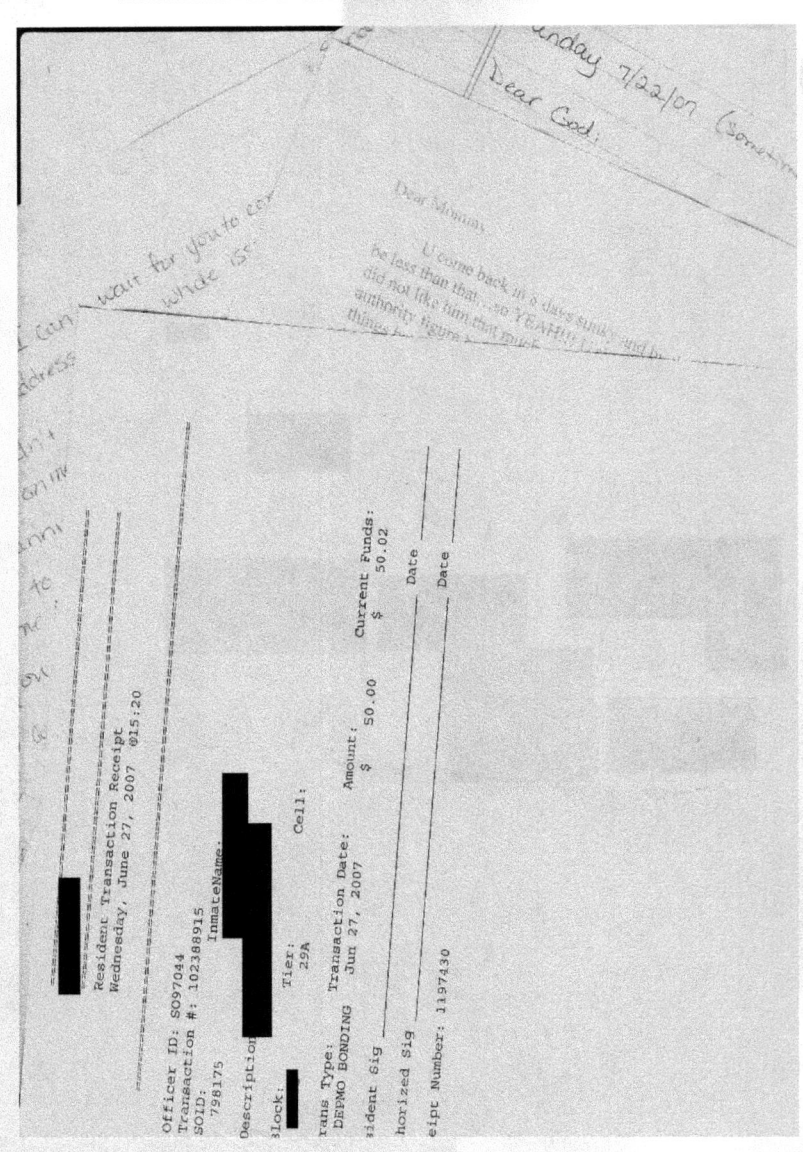

JAILED BY BLOOD: INMATE 798175

JAILED BY BLOOD: INMATE 798175

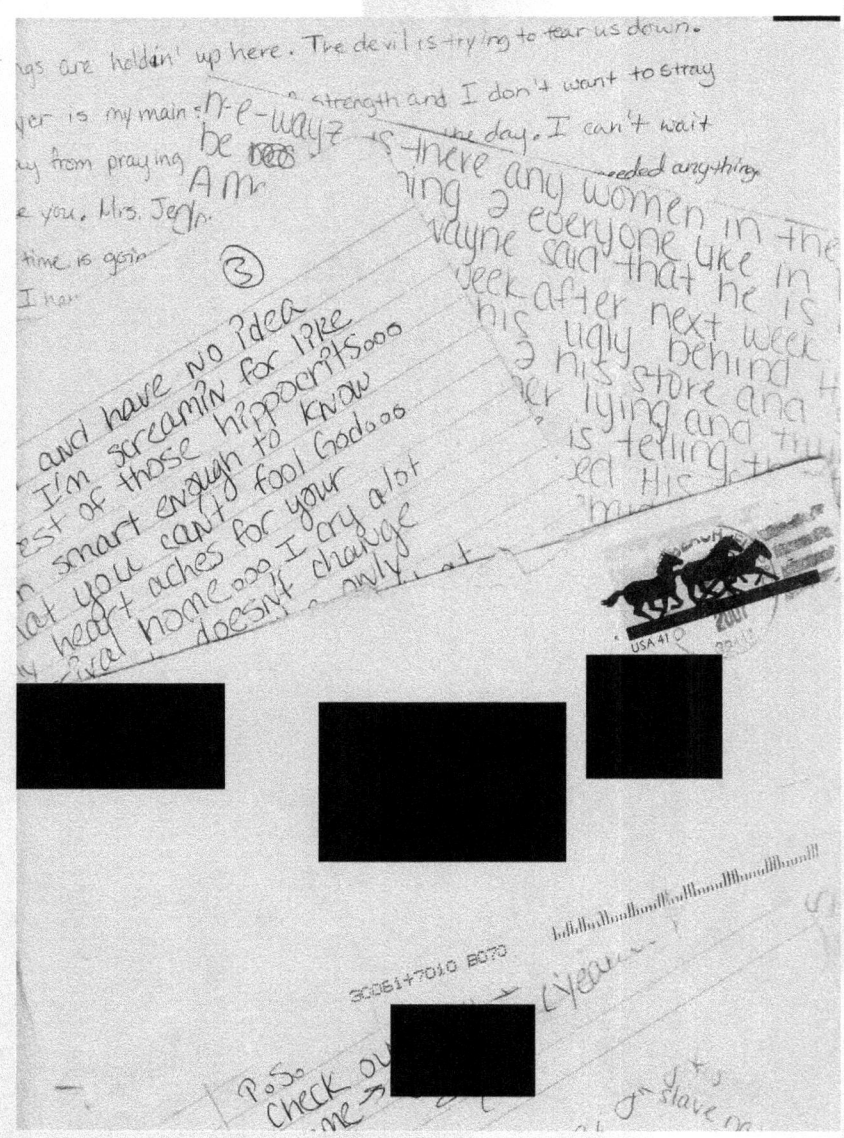

~ Isaiah 54:17

No weapon that is formed against thee shall prosper; and every tongue that shall rise against thee in judgment thou shalt condemn. This is the heritage of the servants of the LORD, and their righteousness is of me, saith the LORD.

www.ingramcontent.com/pod-product-compliance
Lightning Source LLC
Chambersburg PA
CBHW070503100426
42743CB00010B/1745